# Over the Back Fence

Conflicts on the
United States/Canada Border
from Maine to Alaska

# Elizabeth Tower

Since 1978

PO Box 221974 Anchorage, Alaska 99522-1974
books@publicationconsultants.com—www.publicationconsultants.com

ISBN 978-1-59433-112-1

Library of Congress Catalog Card Number: 2009936111

Manufactured in the United States of America.

# Dedication

*Over the Back Fence* is dedicated to Canadian historians Pierre Berton and Peter Newman who made history live and convinced me that North American history is not limited by boundaries of the United States of America.

# Contents

# Foreword

I am an American and for more than fifty years an Alaskan. As an Alaskan I have more contact with Canada than many Americans, because I pass through that foreign country whenever I drive to any of the south 48 states, or even to Southeastern Alaska. When driving through Whitehorse in Yukon Territory, I always stop at Mac's Fireweed bookstore to pick up Canadian books, which are difficult to find in U.S. bookstores. Some of these Canadian books, notably Pierre Berton's two-volume history of the War of 1812 and Peter Newman's three-volume history of the Hudson's Bay Company have made me realize that there is a lot of North American history that I did not learn in school. That history, which centers around the United States-Canada border, explains in part why Americans and Canadians are different. They share the ties of common blood, they look alike, sometimes talk alike, and even drive on the same side of the road, but they don't always think alike. Pierre Berton has summed up these differences: "Three words—*loyalty, security*, and *order*—took on a Canadian connotation. *Freedom*, tossed about like a cricket ball by all sides, had a special meaning, too: it meant freedom from the United States. *Liberty* was exclusively American, never used north of the border, perhaps because it was too close to libertine for the pious Canadians. Radicalism was the opposite of *loyalty*, democracy the opposite of *order*." I am writing this book because there is no better way to understand the difference between Canadians and Americans than to read the story of the historical conflicts along the U.S.-Canada border.

The United States has generally fared well in the resolution of disputed territory, which resulted from lack of geographical knowledge and inaccurate maps. Some of the temperate territory granted to the

United States might have been of greater value to Canada because most Canadians choose to live within a hundred miles of the border. The United States had a head start because it was an organized country with a concept of manifest destiny while Canada was still separate British crown colonies and a huge quasi-governmental commercial enterprise. Once the Canada colonies confederated and acquired Rupert's Land from the Hudson's Bay Company, the Dominion of Canada developed its own form of manifest destiny. However, Great Britain controlled Canada's foreign relations until after World War II. At the time that some of the boundary conflicts were resolved, Great Britain was more anxious to stay in the good graces of the United States, a most valuable trading partner, than to foster the manifest destiny of Canada.

In spite of its turbulent history, the U.S.-Canada border has become a happy place where residents of both countries enjoy a symbiotic existence. May it always continue to be so.

# American Revolution—Treaty of Paris

In the United States the conflict lasting from 1776 to 1783 is known as the American Revolution or the War for Independence. Some Canadians prefer to refer to it as the First American Civil War. In many ways it was a civil war because the people of the rebelling colonies were divided in loyalties. Although exact numbers are not known, an estimated 90,000, 30% of the population, were still loyal to Great Britain and many more colonists remained neutral during the war. The Loyalists included tenant farmers in the middle Atlantic colonies, highland Scots in the Carolinas, Anglican clergy and their parishioners, and a few Presbyterians in the southern colonies. A large number of Iroquois Indians stayed loyal to the king, but Germans and Quakers in Pennsylvania preferred to remain neutral, fearing that joining the revolution would jeopardize their royal land grants.

Colonists who refused to renounce their loyalty to King George III were often shunned by their neighbors and sometimes subjected to torture such as tar and feathering. Patriots would strip the Loyalist of his clothing and make him watch the tar boiling. Then they would pour tar over the Loyalist and make him roll in feathers. Tar was hard to clean off and blistered the skin which usually came off with the tar. Loyalist property was confiscated and many were forced to leave homes, businesses and farms. Some Loyalists joined British troops in the area or formed Loyalist militia units. The vast majority of Loyalists remained in America during and after the war and some who had fled to Europe eventually returned. About 70,000 Loyalists went to present day Canada, 32,000 to Nova Scotia, where the colony of New Brunswick was created for them in 1784. Others arrived in the eastern townships of Quebec where the governor of Quebec provided land for them in the area which became known as Upper Canada, and later Ontario. These British sympathizers were the first of Canada's political refugees and the first true British settlers since previously Lower Canada had been predominately French.

The influence of the Loyalists on the evolution of Canada has persisted. Their ties with Great Britain and their antipathy to the United States has provided strength to keep Canada independent in North America. The Loyalists' distrust of republicanism has influenced Canada's gradual path to independence. The Canada provinces of New Brunswick and Ontario were founded as places of refuge for the United Empire Loyalists.

After the American Revolution, there were two countries involved rather than two British colonies, and the exact boundaries of the United States of America with British Canada became of increased importance. As was the custom of the times, all important negotiations involving North America took place thousands of miles away in Europe, involving long ocean voyages for the new Americans. Preliminary peace negotiations began in Paris in the second half of 1782. In a letter to James Sullivan, John Adams pointed out that the Mitchell Map was the only one that the ministers plenipotentiary of the United States and Great Britain used in discussion relative to the boundaries of the United States. Various copies of Mitchell Maps have subsequently appeared in archives of different countries with red lines drawn to indicate possible borders. Some of these maps were used in later deliberations, but at the time the negotiators realized their inaccuracies in respect to areas that had not been well explored. Therefore, the Treaty of Paris, signed on September 3, 1783 by John Adams, John Jay and Benjamin Franklin, representing the United States of America, and David Hartley, a member of the British Parliament representing King George III, contained only this verbal description of the colonial boundaries:

> From the northwest angle of Nova Scotia, viz. that angle which is formed by a line drawn due north from the source of Saint Croix River to the Highlands; along the said Highlands which divide those rivers that empty themselves into the St. Lawrence, from

those which fall into the Atlantic Ocean, to the northwesternmost head of Connecticut River; thence down along the middle of that river, to the forty-fifth degree of north latitude; from thence, by a line due west on said latitude, until it strikes the river Iroquois or Cataraquy; thence along the middle of said river into Lake Ontario, through the middle of said lake until it strikes the communication by water between that lake and Lake Erie; thence along the middle of said communication into Lake Erie, through the middle of said lake until it arrives at the water communication between that lake and Lake Huron; thence through the middle of the communication by water between that lake and Lake Huron; thence along the middle of said lake until it arrives at the water communication between that lake and Lake Superior; thence through the middle of Lake Superior northward of the Isles Royal and Phelipeaux, to the Long Lake; thence through the middle of Long Lake, and the water communication between it and the Lake of the Woods, to the said Lake of the Woods; thence through the said lake to the most northwestern point thereof, and from thence on a due west course to the river Mississippi; thence by a line to be drawn along the middle of the said river Mississippi until it shall intersect the northwesternmost part of the thirty-first degree of north latitude.

South, by a line to be drawn due east from the determination of the line last mentioned, in the latitude of thirty-one degrees north of the Equator, to the middle of the river Apalachicola or Catahouche; thence along the middle thereof to its junction with the Flint river; thence straight to the head of St. Mary's River; and thence down along the middle of St. Mary's River to the Atlantic Ocean.

East, by a line drawn along the middle of the river St. Croix, from its mouth in the Bay of Fundy to its source, and from its source directly north to the aforesaid Highlands, which divide the rivers that fall into the Atlantic Ocean from those which fall into the river St. Lawrence; comprehending all islands within twenty leagues of any part of the shores of the United States, and lying between lines to be drawn due east from the points where the aforesaid boundaries between Nova Scotia on the one part, and East Florida

on the other, shall respectively touch the Bay of Fundy and the Atlantic Ocean, excepting such as now are, or heretofore have been,
within the limits of the said province of Nova Scotia.

This ponderous description of the border still left uncertain-
ties which remained open to partisan interpretation, particularly
in regard to the boundary between Massachusetts/Maine and New
Brunswick and Quebec. None of the rivers draining into the Bay
of Fundy were currently called the St. Croix, location of "the highlands" was uncertain, and the exact source of the Connecticut River
was yet to be determined. Furthermore, negotiators of the Treaty of
Paris did not suspect that the source of the Mississippi River (Lake
Itasca) was south of the northwesternmost point of the Lake of the
Woods. These geographical inaccuracies were to cause future conflict
and anomalies in the location of the International Border.

Additional terms of the Treaty of Paris included recognition of the
13 colonies as free and sovereign States; granting of fishing rights to
United States fishermen in the Grand Banks off the coast of Newfoundland; restitution of confiscated estates, rights, and properties
belonging to Loyalists and prevention of future confiscation; and
perpetual access to the Mississippi River for Great Britain and the
United States.

Over the ensuing ten years several issues arose, necessitating further diplomatic negotiation between the United States and Great
Britain. The French Revolution had caused both Great Britain and
the United States to want to improve trade relations. Since Great
Britain was fearful of war with France, it was particularly anxious
to assure the continued neutrality of the United States. The United
States protested that Great Britain had not removed troops from military outposts in the Northwest Territory of the United States and
accused the British of inciting Native American attacks on settlers.
Furthermore, the boundary between the United States and Canada
needed further delineation. The United States had not honored the
provision to pay reparations for property confiscated from the Loyalists. John Jay served as the chief negotiator for the United States and
the resulting agreement is known as the Jay Treaty or the Treaty of
London of 1794. Again the negotiations regarding America occurred
in Europe. No definite resolution regarding the border was arrived

at, but a commission was appointed to determine the identity of the St. Croix River.

The appointed commission visited the rivers draining into the Bay of Fundy and managed to identify some ruins from the original colony that Champlain founded in the early 1600s. As a result, they identified the river, now known as the St. Croix, as lying west of the Magaguadavik River which the Americans had considered to be the St. Croix referred to in the Treaty of Paris. Thus the Jay Treaty established the eastern boundary between Massachusetts (now Maine) and New Brunswick but there remained controversy regarding the location of the "highlands."

Treaty of Paris (unfinished painting—from left to right) John Jay, John Adams, Benjamin Franklin, Henry Laurens, and William Temple Franklin. The British commissioners refused to pose and the painting was never finished. *circa 1783*

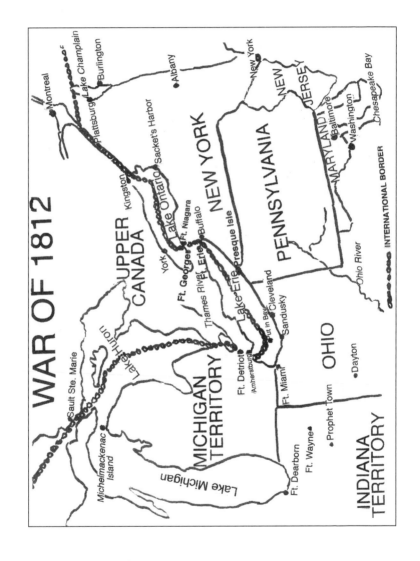

WAR OF 1812

# War of 1812

The United States of America and Great Britain enjoyed relative peace for 18 years following the signing of the Jay Treaty. More land to the west became available to the United States in 1803 when President Thomas Jefferson arranged purchase of the Louisiana Territory from France. As Americans moved into the western lands conflict with Indian tribes was inevitable. Some tribes willingly sold land to the American land companies, which then made parcels available for settlement. This practice allowed Ohio to attain sufficient population to become a state in 1804.

In the adjoining Indiana Territory, Territorial Governor William Henry Harrison attempted to buy land from the Miami tribe, but received protests from other tribes, particularly the Shawnee and their chief Tecumseh, who wished to consolidate tribes into an Indian nation. Tecumseh's negotiations with Harrison were largely peaceful until the summer of 1811. While Tecumseh was away attempting to persuade southern tribes to join his confederation, Harrison moved troops to threaten Prophet's Town, the village of Tecumseh's brother. The Battle of Tippecanoe ensued when some of the Indians disobeyed Tecumseh's orders and attacked Harrison's troops. The Indians retreated and abandoned the town when they ran out of ammunition. Two days later Harrison's troops ravaged and plundered Prophet's Town, even destroying stores of corn and beans. Rather than teaching the Indians a lesson and pacifying them, raids on settlers intensified and the Indians increased their dependence on the British for weapons.

Harrison proclaimed the Battle of Tippecanoe a great victory for the Americans and a personal triumph that eventually helped earn him the presidency of the United States. In doing so, he greatly exaggerated the Indian losses. Some consider the Battle of Tippecanoe to be the first conflict of the War of 1812.

Meanwhile, the Napoleonic War raged in Europe. The French army and navy threatened Great Britain on land and sea. The British, still considering American colonists to be of British origin stopped American ships at sea to recover defecting British seamen, and even impressing some Americans to fill their need for additional sailors. During 1812, nineteen sailors who claimed American citizenship were detained by the British navy but only two were taken from their ships. Furthermore, the British enacted the Orders in Council, a series of edicts that blockaded continental ports and barred foreign ships from them unless they first called at a British port and paid customs duties.

Americans resented the boarding of their ships and the restrictions to trade caused by the Orders in Council. A group of young men in the House of Representatives, led by Henry Clay of Kentucky and John Calhoun of South Carolina, favored punishing Great Britain for its lack of respect for United States' sovereignty. These activists, referred to as War Hawks, promoted war with Great Britain in the hope of taking over the remaining British North American colonies. In an early declaration of "manifest destiny," Clay announced, "I am not for stopping at Quebec or anywhere else, but I would take the whole continent from them and ask no favors." Since a considerable number of Americans had moved into Upper Canada to take advantage of the offer of free land, even Thomas Jefferson had stated that the mere presence of American troops across the border would be enough to make Upper Canada wish to join the United States.

On June 18, 1812, two days after the British Parliament announced plans to renounce the Orders in Council and five days before it actually did so, President James Madison signed the declaration of war with Great Britain. The ensuing conflict is known in the United States as the War of 1812 or the Second American War for Independence. Across the border, it was simply the invasion of Canada.

Invading Canada in 1812 appeared to be a comparatively easy conquest for the United States, which had a population of about seven and a half million as compared to a total of 500,000 people in Canada. A full third of the 100,000 residents of Upper Canada were American by birth or descent. Governor Daniel Tompkins of New York confidently predicted that one-half of the militia in Canada would join the

United States forces. Neither country was well prepared for war. The United States was relying on aging officers who had participated in the Revolutionary War as young men. The cream of the British officer corps was involved in fighting Napoleon in Europe. Anticipating war, the United States had devised a plan to invade Canada on three fronts. Initially the Americans would attack through Detroit and capture the British fort at Amherstburg. This invasion would coordinate with one on the Niagara peninsula, and eventually, Montreal would be attacked through the corridor up from Lake Champlain.

Madison needed an experienced general to lead the northwestern portion of the proposed invasion of Canada and settled on fifty-nine-year-old William Hull, the governor of the Michigan Territory, who had been a lieutenant-colonel in the Revolutionary War. Hull, over-weight and accustomed to a life of leisure, reluctantly accepted and was appointed a brigadier general. Although he was not concerned with the impressment of seamen, Hull was worried about the British alliance with Indian tribes that were harassing settlers in the western territories. His worries were well founded. Since communications were difficult, word of the declaration of war did not reach the American fort at Michilmackinac Island between Lake Huron and Lake Michigan until after the British, with Indian help, captured it on July 17, 1812, a full month after the start of war. All the territory west of the American fort at Detroit was, therefore, already under British and Indian control.

Hull, who set out for Detroit in early June, met twelve hundred Ohio militia soldiers, recruited by Ohio Governor, Return Meigs. The men arriving at Dayton were dressed in tattered homespun clothes and carried an assortment of battered weapons. Three hundred regular army troops from the Fourth U.S. Regiment joined Hull at Urbana in western Ohio. A letter from Secretary of War William Eustis, which had been written prior to the declaration of war, reached Hull on June 27, telling him to proceed to Detroit. When the troops reached the Maumee River, they encountered the packet boat *Cuyahoga* anchored along the bank. Hull, who did not realize that the United States was already at war with the British, decided that this boat would be a safe way to send ailing troops and supplies to Detroit. He sent his son, Captain Abraham Hull, on the boat with a trunk containing the secret muster rolls of American troops and his private instructions from Washington. The British at Amherstburg, who had heard about the declaration of war, seized the *Cuyahoga* and the trunk with Hull's military intelligence. A letter informing Hull that the war had begun did not reach him until July 2 because it was sent by public mail and had gone through post offices at Buffalo, Cleveland and Sandusky before reaching the troops. General Isaac Brock, the Governor of Upper Canada, located at York, the site of modern Toronto, thus understood Hull's plan and was prepared to reinforce Fort Malden at Amherstburg.

Hull arrived at Fort Detroit on July 5, but his attempts to cross the Detroit River to advance on Amherstburg were delayed a week because some of the Ohio militia refused to enter a foreign country. When he finally landed in Canada, unopposed, with the Fourth Infantry Regiment, Hull issued a proclamation inviting the inhabitants to join him, stating "Inhabitants of Canada! You will be emancipated from tyranny and oppression and restored to the dignified status of freemen." Most Canadians, even those recently arrived from the United States, already enjoyed considerable freedom and did not wish to take advantage of the invitation to join the invading Americans. The Canada militia and the Indians disappeared into the woodlands awaiting a coordinated attack with General Brock. Hull advanced toward Fort Malden but delayed the siege because he was concerned about his supply lines and was awaiting General Henry Dearborn's attack on the Niagara frontier. A detachment sent to meet a supply train sent from Ohio was attacked by Tecumseh and his Indians at the Raisin River 35 miles south of Detroit.

When Hull learned that the British had captured the American fort at Mackinac Island, he felt that he was surrounded by potentially hostile Indians. Then, when he learned that a British force was approaching by boat on Lake Erie, Hull and his invading army retreated back to the safety of Fort Detroit.

General Isaac Brock was more of a gambler than Hull. Since the Americans had not advanced on the Niagara frontier, he felt that, with the British navy in control of Lake Erie, he could move some of the troops from Fort George along the northern shore of Lake Erie to support Fort Malden at Amherstburg where he joined Tecumseh and his Indians. The British landed cannon and mortars across the river from Detroit and began shelling the American fort. Taking advantage of Hull's timidity, Brock sent a message on August 15 demanding surrender of Fort Detroit. "It is far from my intention to join in a war of extermination," he wrote, "but you must be aware that the numerous body of Indians who have attached themselves to my troops, will be beyond control the moment the contest commences." This was not an exaggerated warning. The Americans that Hull had ordered to abandon Fort Dearborn, the site of modern Chicago, had been attacked and murdered by Indians on their way to Detroit.

Hull initially refused the demand, but Brock used psychological warfare to capitalize on Hull's fears. He dressed the Canada militia in red shirts to make them look like regular British troops, and instructed the Indians to parade through the woods repeatedly in single file so that there appeared to be a large force of Indians. The following day, when a cannonball crashed into the officer's mess, Hull sent his son across the river under a flag of truce to accept Brock's terms, and promptly surrendered his entire army. At noon on August 16, a British column marched into Fort Detroit with Brock at its head. Hull was captured, but later returned to the United States on parole, as was the customary practice with captured officers who agreed not to engage in future hostilities. He was subsequently court-martialed and convicted of cowardice and neglect of duty. Hull contended that he was the victim of the War Department's ineptitude because Brock was able oppose him at Detroit instead of fighting the American troops that were supposed to attack the British on the Niagara peninsula.

Americans had not invaded Canada on the Niagara peninsula because Canada's Governor General Sir George Prevost had sent an envoy to General Henry Dearborn suggesting a cease fire, which had taken effect on August 20. Prevost was not as eager to fight as Brock and had cautioned Brock repeatedly to fight a defensive war rather than further antagonizing the Americans by aggressive action. The Americans welcomed this temporary cease fire because it gave them an opportunity to increase troops and weapons on the Niagara front. Although the terms of the cease fire forbid movement of troops, the Americans managed to make General Roger Sheaffe, who was commanding the troops on the Niagara front while Brock was at Detroit, agree to allow the Americans to have free transportation on Lake Ontario.

Euphoric after his capture of Detroit, General Brock was hurrying back to his capital at York when a provincial schooner stopped his boat on August 23 with news of the cease fire on the Niagara frontier. He was mortified because he had hoped to continue the momentum of his victory while the Americans on Lake Ontario were still poorly prepared. He was enthusiastically greeted at York and went on to Kingston at the east end of Lake Ontario where he was hailed as the Savior of Upper Canada. Then Brock hurried back to Fort George at the top of the Niagara peninsula to prepare for an expected American attack when the cease fire was due to end on September 8. He was chagrined to realize that the Americans had succeeded in reinforcing their army during the armistice and sent word to Detroit and Kingston to send more troops to Fort George. Although Brock still wanted to attack the Americans across the Niagara River, Prevost argued that Britain was only interested in fighting a defensive war on the American front while also engaged in fighting Napoleon in Europe. On September 9, the day after the armistice ended, Napoleon won the Battle of Borodino and prepared to invade Russia. The casualties on that day exceeded 80,000, about equal to the population of Upper Canada.

General Dearborn at Albany still wavered, expecting the British to attack. The weather was stormy and many of the Americans on the Niagara peninsula were too sick with dysentery to fight. In early October, General Stephen Van Rensselaer, encamped at Lewiston in the center of the Niagara Peninsula with the bulk of the American army, received an ultimatum from his troops. They warned the general that they would go home if he didn't take the offensive. Van Rensselaer, therefore, planned a night landing across the river on October 11. However, missed connections resulted in thirteen boats, each able to carry twenty-five men, having no oars. Two days later at 3AM, the Americans attacked the British at Queenston. The attack was poorly coordinated, but some Americans succeeded in capturing high ground and killing General Brock in the heat of battle while he was at the head of his troops. General Sheaffe arrived with Mohawk Indians to take charge after Brock was killed. The New York militia refused to cross the river to reinforce the beachhead so the Americans were forced to retreat. While Lieutenant Colonel Winfield Scott was attempting to cover the retreat of American troops under attack by Indians, he was captured and taken to General Sheaffe. Although Scott urged Sheaffe to let him go and share the fate of his troops, Sheaffe protected him from the Indians. Sheaffe, himself, was appalled at the slaughter by the Indians. The British took 925 American prisoners, including a brigadier general, five lieutenant colonels and 67 other officers. In addition the Americans suffered about 250 casualties. The British lost only 14 killed and 77 wounded. Nothing, however, could compensate for the loss of General Isaac Brock. All of Canada mourned Brock, and his body lay in state for three days. Even though he was a British officer, he would become the first Canada war hero. A monument, erected on the site where he fell, became a symbol of the Loyalist way as opposed to the Yankee way.

The American attack had failed on all three fronts. Detroit was occupied by the British, and an American army sent to retake the fort was attacked and slaughtered by Indians at the Raisin River. The offensive on the Niagara peninsula was poorly handled. Americans did not attempt to attack Montreal because General Dearborn was unable to interest the New England states in raising militias and participating in the war. The only bright spot for the Americans in 1812 was the naval victory of the *Constitution*, affectionately called "old Ironside" over the British vessel *Guerriere*. When Captain Isaac Hull, nephew of the defeated general, reported his victory and landed his prisoners in Boston, New Englanders rallied around "old ironsides" and its crew. Hull's victory had political ramifications as well and President James Madison was elected to a second four-year term. Meanwhile, in Europe, Napoleon was retreating from Moscow. The war in Europe was beginning to turn in favor of the British and their allies.

Madison started his new term by appointing General John Armstrong to replace Eustis as secretary of war. It was now apparent to the Americans that control of the lakes was essential to any victory. Captain Isaac Chauncey was made a commodore and dispatched to Sacket's Harbor on the eastern end of Lake Ontario with 700 seamen and 140 ship's carpenters to build two fighting ships, each with 32 guns. The British were also building big ships, one at Kingston on the east end of Lake Ontario and another at York. On Lake Erie, the Americans decided to use Presque Island Bay near Erie, Pennsylvania, as the site to build two 20-gun warships and several gunboats. The British were building an even larger ship at Amherstburg.

General Dearborn, the portly 61-year-old commander that his troops called "Granny," remained in charge of the central American army at Albany. As 1813 began, the Americans again made plans to attack Canada. With Detroit in British control, they planned to take charge on Lake Ontario with attacks at Kingston and Niagara. Capture of Kingston would lead to control of the entrance to the

St. Lawrence seaway, but Dearborn decided that the Upper Canada capital York would be an easier target. York had no strategic value, but Dearborn hoped that Americans might capture the ship that was under construction in the unprotected harbor there. The previous year, American seamen had succeeded in capturing two British ships near Fort Erie on Lake Erie. Capturing ships was quicker and easier than building them because, with British controlling the St. Lawrence seaway, the Americans had to transport building materials overland through undeveloped wilderness to reach the lakes.

Commodore Chauncey left Sacket's Harbor on April 25, 1813 with 1500 army regulars under the command of Brigadier General Zebulon Pike, who had previously led an exploratory expedition into the Rocky Mountains. On the morning of April 27, Pike watched his troops land at York. They met little resistance because British General Sheaffe, realizing that he could not hold the capital, had retreated to Kingston with the regular troops. Before leaving, the British detonated an underground magazine containing barrels of gunpowder. The resulting explosion killed many American soldiers including General Pike, who was hit by a falling boulder. Although the British burned the large ship that was under construction, Americans managed to capture supplies of food and ship-building materials. The terms of surrender indicated that British property would not be destroyed, however, American troops angered the Canadian settlers by burning all the government buildings and pillaging private homes.

The American troops then successfully attacked Fort George and Fort Erie on the Niagara peninsula. Colonel Winfield Scott, who had been taken prisoner at the Battle of Queenston the previous year, appeared again as adjutant to General Dearborn, although he had agreed not to take part in future hostilities. Since the British did not have facilities to house prisoners, they usually only imprisoned American soldiers until they could be exchanged for British soldiers of equal value. Scott apparently had not honored this commitment to stay out of the fight. While the British soldiers under the command of Brigadier General John Vincent were retreating from Fort George, Vincent's adjutant, Colonel John Harvey, successfully repelled the Americans at the Battle of Stony Creek. The Americans then abandoned Fort Erie and left the American troops at Fort George surrounded by British. Aside from occasional skirmishes, the armies on the Niagara peninsula were deadlocked for the rest of the summer.

At Presque Isle on Lake Erie, Americans were making good progress on the twin warships, *Lawrence* and *Niagara*. The British at Amherstburg were having difficulty building the large ship *Detroit* because the supplies that the Americans had taken at York were not available. Furthermore, both Amherstburg and Fort Detroit were short of food. On August 1, the two 20-gun American warships were ready for service. In order to get the new ships into open water they had to strip them down and kedge them over the bar protecting the Presque Isle harbor by pulling them to dropped anchors. This accomplished, the ships were refurbished. Commodore Oliver Hazard Perry took command of the flagship *Lawrence* and Captain Jesse Duncan Elliot commanded the *Niagara*.

The American ships waited at Put-in Bay in the Bass Islands near Sandusky for Captain Robert Heriot Barclay to emerge from Amherstburg in his new flagship *Detroit*. Eventually Barclay, although ill-prepared, was forced to challenge the Americans because of the shortage of food at Amherstburg. The Battle of Lake Erie began on September 10, 1813, with nine American ships and gunboats facing six British ships. Early in the fight, the *Lawrence* joined battle with the *Detroit* and was disabled. Perry was able to transfer to the *Niagara* and win the naval engagement when Barclay, aboard the disabled *Detroit*, surrendered. Perry's terse message to General William Henry Harrison with the American army at Fort Meigs in Ohio simply stated, "We have met the enemy and they are ours." With capture of the British fleet, Americans gained control of Lake Erie. Harrison's army was then transported to retake Fort Detroit.

The British troops, commanded by General Henry Procter, decided to retreat up the Thames valley along the south shore of Lake St. Clair and were pursued by Harrison's troops. Tecumseh and the Indians disapproved of Procter's retreat, but joined the British when the armies faced each other in the Battle of the Thames in early October. Harrison's army prevailed and Procter fled eastward, only to face court martial for delaying his retreat too long after the naval defeat and failing to choose a suitable place to make his stand. Casualties, though relatively small on both sides, were crucial because the Indian leader Tecumseh was killed. With the death of Tecumseh, all hopes for an Indian Confederacy also died. American troops pillaged and burned farms and villages in Upper Canada so Indian and settlers were forced to beg for food.

Flush with victory, the American troops made plans to move on to the east and attack either Kingston or Montreal. General Dearborn had been replaced by General James Wilkinson, who had a checkered career that included support of Aaron Burr in his attempt to form an independent country in the American west and service as a Spanish agent. Wilkinson agreed to a plan to attack Montreal as long as the army based at Lake Champlain under the command of General Wade Hampton would participate by attacking the British army in the St. Lawrence valley. Hampton refused to take orders from Wilkinson, but agreed to the plan as long as the orders were given by Secretary of War Armstrong. Hampton crossed the border and advanced along the Chateauguay River until he encountered Canadian troops under the command of Lieutenant Colonel Charles de Salaberry, a French Canadian commissioned as a regular officer in the British Army. A short battle ensued in which Hampton over-estimated the strength of the opposition and decided that retreat was his only option. Wilkinson's army proceeded up the St. Lawrence River until November 11, when it encountered two British divisions that held their ground and moved forward with bayonets fixed. The Americans retreated and Wilkinson decided to abandon the attack on Montreal and go into winter camp at French Mills on the U.S.-Canada border. Wilkinson blamed Hampton for the failure to capture Montreal.

Fort George had been left short handed when most of the troops stationed there joined the proposed attack on Montreal. New York militia general George McClure, who was left in charge of Fort George, decided to withdraw his 250 soldiers across the river to Fort Niagara. Before they left, the American soldiers completely burned the nearby Canada village of Newark, forcing four hundred civilians, mostly women and children, to escape in a blinding snow storm. When British troops and Canada militia arrived on the scene, they vowed revenge. On December 18, they captured Fort Niagara, killing 67 Americans and taking 350 prisoners. To avenge the burning of Newark, the British burned the American towns of Black Rock and Buffalo to the ground on December 30. Only three buildings were left standing in Buffalo. As a reprisal for the burning of Buffalo, the Americans under Lieutenant Colonel John B. Campbell attacked and destroyed Port Dover on the north shore of Lake Erie on May 15, 1814. Campbell was reprimanded by a court of inquiry, but it did not appease the British who had another wanton act to avenge.

Although they hesitated to attempt to attack Montreal again, the Americans still hoped to conquer Upper Canada. Major General Jacob Brown replaced Wilkinson as head of the army and Winfield Scott, newly commissioned a brigadier general at the age of twenty-eight, was one of his new brigade commanders. On July 3, 1814, Scott led his brigade across the Niagara River in small boats. Two additional brigades promptly joined him, and they captured Fort Erie. British Major General Rial moved troops south from Fort George to counter the American advance and formed a defensive line along the Chippawa River two miles from Niagara falls. When the armies met two days later, Scott's brigade held their ground. The Americans could finally proclaim victory against British regular troops. Young General Winfield Scott joined the naval commanders as American heroes.

General Brown moved his entire army across the Niagara River. He planned to link up with Commodore Chauncey and his ships for an assault on Fort George and then march westward around Lake Ontario to capture York. Chauncey, however, refused to cooperate. He replied to Brown that his fleet had been created to fight the British fleet and should not be diverted to assist the army. In the meantime, the British reinforced their troops, which were now under the command of Lieutenant General Gordon Drummond, who had served with the Duke of Wellington. The armies met in the Battle of Lundy's Lane, in which both generals Brown and Scott were wounded. Brigadier General Eleazer Ripley assumed command and withdrew his American troops from the field early on the morning of July 26. General Drummond, who was also wounded, was content to let the Americans retreat to Fort Erie. The British subsequently attempted unsuccessfully to retake Fort Erie during the remainder of the summer. In spite of arguments about which side won the Battle of Lundy's Lane, Drummond's stand had halted Brown's drive up the Niagara peninsula and ended any hope that Americans would conquer Upper Canada. On November 5, 1814, Major General George Izard, who replaced General Brown, ordered all American troops to evacuate the Canada side of the Niagara peninsula. As they left, the Americans blew up Fort Erie.

As soon as Napoleon was defeated in Europe and exiled to Elba, Great Britain sent more ships and war-tested soldiers to fight in North America. The British navy, under the command of Vice Admiral Sir Alexander Forester Inglis Cochrane completely blockaded the east coast of the United States and entered Chesapeake Bay, attacking American ships and coastal villages. Cochrane's intent to deliver retribution along the American coast was intensified by a July memo from Governor General Prevost asking for retaliation for the American attack on Long Point. A brigade of Wellington's veterans, under the command of Major General Robert Ross, was dispatched to aid Cochrane. Ross was initially instructed to effect a diversion along the coast while Prevost, with three veteran brigades invaded the United States through Plattsburgh and Lake Champlain. On August 15, the transports carrying Ross's brigade of about 3400 men sailed into Chesapeake Bay to join Cochrane and Admiral George Cockburn, who had a reputation for burning American property. Ross and his troops disembarked at Benedict on the upper Patuxent River on August 19 and moved north toward Washington. Secretary of War Armstrong had not made plans to defend Washington and most of the regular American troops were fighting on other fronts, so Brigadier General William Winder had to rely on Maryland militia. President Madison, Secretary of State James Monroe and Secretary of War Armstrong were on the battlefield as British troops crossed the Bladensburg bridge seven miles north of Washington. At twilight General Ross and Admiral Cockburn rode boldly down Maryland Avenue to the east side of the Capitol. No American government officials were present to negotiate a truce and soon the Capitol, the presidential mansion, and other government buildings were ablaze. The following afternoon as Washington burned, a violent thunderstorm struck, partially extinguishing the flames. On the evening of August 25, Ross ordered the troops to withdraw and they departed hastily to Benedict and the waiting British ships.

On September 7, Admiral Cochrane decided to attack Baltimore, less than 40 miles northeast of Washington. Major General Samuel Smith of the Maryland militia had prepared for the defense of Baltimore. He assembled about 9000 militiamen in and around the city and dug an elaborate system of earthworks. Central to the defense of Baltimore was Fort McHenry sitting on a small peninsula between branches of the Patapsco River. The shallow depth of the river prevented larger vessels entering the harbor so Cochrane landed General Ross with about 4000 soldiers at North Pointe to advance on Baltimore by land. Admiral Cockburn accompanied Ross as he had during the attack on Washington. After marching 14 miles without meeting resistance, the British troops encountered the first line of militia and realized that they were facing a larger than expected force. General Ross was riding back to alert his reserves when a sniper's bullet struck him in the chest inflicting a mortal wound. The British troops, advised not to charge the earthworks unless they were sure of success, left their campfires burning and retreated to the ships, Fort McHenry held out through a night of bombardment and Admiral Cochrane decided that the capture of Baltimore would not be worth further loss. The next day with favorable winds, the British fleet sailed out of Chesapeake Bay. The British attack on Baltimore has been memorable primarily because an American lawyer named Francis Scott Key composed a poem that became the words of the American national anthem while watching the bombardment of Fort McHenry.

Admiral Cochrane succeeded in accomplishing the requested diversion and the time had come for Governor General George Prevost in Montreal to make his move. On June 3, 1814, the Earl of Bathurst, secretary of state for war and the colonies, sent Prevost his marching orders. With the addition of ten thousand veteran infantry and three artillery companies, Prevost was ordered to take the offensive. His objectives were the recapture of Detroit and the gaining of naval superiority on Lake Erie and Lake Champlain. Since Vermont farmers were providing food to feed the increasing number of British troops, Prevost indicated that he would limit his offensive strike to the New York side of Lake Champlain. The British army crossed the border and, on September 6, reached Plattsburgh and looked out on the lake for naval assistance. The Americans and British had a ship-building race on Lake Champlain like the ones on Lake Erie and Lake Ontario. Master Commandant Thomas Macdonough commanded the newly-built American flagship *Saratoga* and three supporting armed ships, which were anchored in Plattsburgh harbor. The British flagship *Confiance*, equal in size to the *Saratoga*, was nearing completion on the north end of Lake Champlain when Prevost ordered Captain George Downie to coordinate with his troops in attacking Plattsburgh. Downie, who had just been given command of the *Confiance* several days before, sailed down the lake early on the morning of September 11, 1814 with three supporting ships, hoping to engage Macdonough's fleet in open water while Prevost's army attacked the guns defending the harbor. Prevost, however, delayed his attack and Downie encountered the American ships controlling the harbor with no support on land. Lieutenant Henry Robertson, who assumed control of the *Confiance* when Downie was killed, was not able to maneuver his flagship as capably as Macdonough. The British ships were forced to strike colors two hours after the engagement began. Prevost, always more willing to defend than attack, did not feel he could prevail while the Americans controlled the lake. By nightfall, the largest British army ever to march on American soil headed back to Canada. Sir George was replaced as Canada's governor-general and ordered back to England to face court-martial. He died the evening before the hearings were to take place.

As 1814 drew to a close all fronts were relatively calm. The American troops had abandoned the Canada side of the Niagara peninsula and the British armies and navy had retreated from the United States. The border was essentially the same as it was before the United States declared war and attempted to invade Canada. However, the British still occupied the fort on Mackinac Island, which was essential to the fur trade, and part of Massachusetts that in several years would become the state of Maine. Admiral Cochrane was in the West Indies preparing to attack New Orleans which was essential to control of the Louisiana Purchase land.

Politically the United States was in turmoil. The British blockade of the east coast had ruined trade in New England and several northeastern states were considering secession. Representatives of Connecticut, Massachusetts, Rhode Island, Vermont, and New Hampshire met in Hartford on December 15 to discuss the situation. They emerged from the Hartford Conference in early January with recommendations such as requiring a two-thirds vote of both the Senate and the House prior to any future declaration of war. The United States remained intact and further dissension did not occur. Had communications from Europe been swifter, Americans would have known that this unpopular war already had been over for a week.

# Treaty of Ghent

Without the aid of transAtlantic communication, news from Europe took several months to reach the United States. The conflict in North America, therefore, continued for weeks after hostilities should have stopped. The Treaty of Ghent was finally signed by the five representatives from the United States and three from Great Britain on December 24, 1814 in Ghent, Belgium, after months of negotiations

President Madison had been eager to end the War of 1812 almost as soon as it started on the condition that Great Britain would agree to cease the impressment of seamen, but Great Britain was unwilling to make that concession while the British were fighting Napoleon in Europe. After Russia defeated the French at the gates of Moscow, Czar Alexander, in the interest of facilitating trade with both the United States and Britain, offered to mediate the conflict in North America. Madison was glad to accept the offer and appointed a three-man peace commission consisting of John Quincy Adams, James A. Bayard, and Albert Gallatin. Adams was a seasoned diplomat, having served as his father's secretary during negotiations for the Treaty of Paris. Swiss-born Gallatin had served as secretary of the treasury under President Jefferson. The three men traveled to St. Petersburg only to find that the British had not accepted the mediation offer, and that the Czar was with his army in Germany. After six months of waiting, Bayard and Gallatin made plans to visit the Czar and then go to London to sound out the British on direct peace negotiations.

After Napoleon was defeated at Leipzig, Lord Castlereagh, Britain's foreign minister, offered to open direct negotiations. The United States formally accepted the offer on January 5, 1814 and Madison appointed Henry Clay and Jonathan Russell to join the peace delegation. These American negotiators, representing different political parties and varied areas of the United States, presented a strong front. On April 14, Clay and Russell arrived in the ice-choked harbor of Gothenburg, Sweden, but there was no sign of the other three members. Bayard and Gallatin were in London and Adams was icebound on the Gulf of Finland en route from Russia.

Shortly after arriving in Gothenburg, Clay and Russell learned that Paris had fallen. Gallatin reported from London that people there were cheering the end of the war in Europe and hoping to continue fighting in North America to punish to United States. With the war in Europe ending, the British would soon have a seasoned army and navy at their disposal to send across the ocean to join the war.

Lord Castlereagh appointed a three-man British delegation in May, consisting of Admiral Lord Gambier, William Adams, an admiralty lawyer, and Henry Goulburn, an undersecretary for war and the colonies. These men were not equal in stature to the American delegation, and every decision would require direct instruction from London. The peace conference was, therefore, moved to Ghent in Belgium where Castlereagh and Lord Bathurst, the secretary of war and the colonies, could watch negotiations even though they were preoccupied with carving up Napoleon's empire at the Congress of Vienna.

Initially the British proposed an Indian buffer nation between the United States and Canada, consisting of land between the Ohio River and the Great Lakes, and the doctrine of "uti possidetis," which meant that each side could keep whatever it possessed at the end of the war. Although the United States would have dearly loved to acquire land in Canada, the small amount they had at the west end of Lake Erie would not compensate for the British possession of Mackinac Island and land east of the Penobscot River in the future state of Maine, which was also held by the British army. The American delegation immediately refused the creation of the proposed Indian state which would dispossess settlers in the state of Ohio and the Indiana territory. The best the United States could hope for was return to the "ante bellum" land status. Other concerns discussed were continuation of American fishing rights on the Great Banks, a special concern of John Quincy Adams, and navigation rights on the Mississippi River desired by Great Britain. Adams and Clay were at odds over these issues because Clay, a westerner, did not consider the fishing rights as important a consideration as navigation on the Mississippi River. Gallatin was frequently called upon to make peace and to draft proposals that the entire delegation could agree to.

As negotiations proceeded, fighting continued in North America, Washington burned, and the British planned to attack Baltimore, Plattsburgh, and New Orleans. The American delegates suspected that the British were delaying in order to enhance their negotiating position and threatened to go home to America. However, when news that British attacks at Baltimore and Plattsburgh had failed reached Ghent in late October, the British, on the advice of the Duke of Wellington, decided that the "ante bellum" status was agreeable. The British had neither gained nor lost land and the attempted American invasion of Canada had failed. The impressment of American seamen, which was the stated rational of the war, was barely discussed. Several boundary matters, such as ownership of some islands in Passamaquoddy Bay and in rivers connecting the Great Lakes, were left for appointed commissions to decide, as was the northern boundary between New Brunswick and the future state of Maine.

The Treaty of Ghent was signed by the five American and three British delegates on December 24, 1814 and sent on to their respective governments for ratification. In essence, the agreement was that all hostilities would end and "all territory, places, and possessions whatsoever, taken by either party from the other during the war" would be "restored without delay." No mention was made of impressment of seamen, fishing rights, or navigation on the Mississippi River. Neither the Americans nor the British could be called clearcut winners of the War of 1812, but the Indians were definitely losers. The British tried half-heartedly to assert the rights of their Indian allies, but Tecumseh was dead and his dream of an Indian Confederation was gone forever.

Travel across the English Channel was quickly accomplished and the British government formally ratified the Treaty of Ghent on December 28. Travel to the United States was a different matter and would take at least six weeks. In the meantime, Admiral Cochrane was well on his way to attack New Orleans. He sailed from Kingston, Jamaica, with the bulk of his fleet on November 26. General Andrew Jackson, who was in Alabama finishing up a treaty with the Creek Indians, anticipated Cochrane's plan to attack New Orleans and raced to get there in time to defend the city. Cochrane realized that approaching New Orleans would be difficult. The direct route up the tortuous Mississippi River for eighty miles would require passing two American forts. Several land routes across Lake Borgne or Lake Pontchartrain required shallow-draft boats that were in short supply. By the time the British could get their troops in place to attack, Jackson had recruited enough militia to have a force of about four thousand prepared to defend the town.

Just before noon on Christmas day, both sides were improving fortifications when Lieutenant General Sir Edward Pakenham arrived to take command. Pakenham, the brother-in-law of the Duke of Wellington, fought in Europe with the Iron Duke and may have hoped to be governor of Louisiana if the attack succeeded. The British plan was to send a portion of their troops across the Mississippi to bombard the American line from the side while the main army attacked head on. However, the troops crossing the river landed several miles down river and could not get in place in time to aid the attack. Pakenham relied on information about the weakest spot in the American line that may have been planted by a spy. The British ended up attacking an area well reinforced with sharp-shooters that succeeded in killing both Pakenham and Major General Samuel Gibbs, the second in command. Command reverted to Major General John Lambert, who was in the rear with the reserves. Of the three thousand troops in the main British advance, two-thirds were dead or dying. Realizing that he could not hold his line, Lambert ordered retreat. Jackson estimated British losses at 400 killed, 1,400 wounded, and 500 taken prisoner, while reporting only 7 Americans killed and 6 wounded. For nine days after the main battle, the Royal Navy attempted to seize the forts at the mouth of the Mississippi, but the Americans held firm. Both Cochrane and Lambert decided it was time to give up the plan to capture New Orleans. On January 19, 1815, Jackson reported that the enemy had precipitately withdrawn.

Still ignorant of the Treaty of Ghent, Cochrane sailed east and attacked Fort Bowyer on Mobile Bay. The British were tightening the noose around the city of Mobile when Cochrane received word from Jamaica that the war had been over for more than a month. On February 16, the United States Senate acted expeditiously and voted 35-0 to ratify the Treaty of Ghent.

The War of 1812 was over, but there was considerable doubt as to whether any one had won. The victory at New Orleans was hailed in the United States as the penultimate victory, and some American historians have claimed that the War of 1812 succeeded in forging a nation that could stand up to the best of European nations. Secretary of State James Monroe, who followed Madison as president of the United States, proclaimed in an annual message to Congress that the American continents were henceforth not to be considered as subjects for future colonization by any European power.

The doctrine of "manifest destiny" was still alive, but henceforth the United States would look west rather than north to colonize and acquire new land. In his two-volume history of the War of 1812, Canadian historian Pierre Berton pointed out that "the war helped to change Upper Canada from a loose aggregation of village states into something approaching a political entity." Berton concluded: "Thus the war that was supposed to attach the British North American colonies to the United States accomplished exactly the opposite. It ensured that Canada would never become a part of the Union to the south. Because of it, an alternative form of democracy grew out of the British colonial oligarchy in the northern half of the continent. The Canadian 'way'—so difficult to define except in terms of negatives-- has its roots in the invasion of 1812-1814, the last American invasion of Canada. There can never be another."

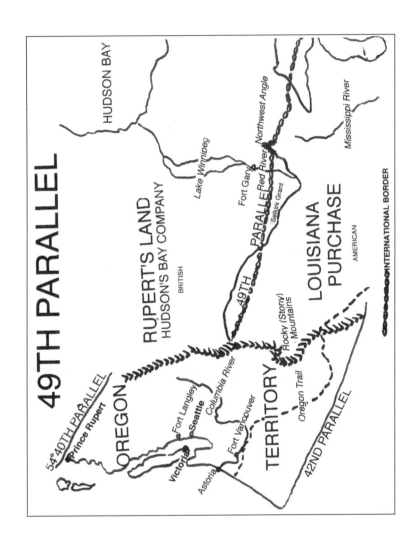

# The Forty-Ninth Parallel

The Treaty of Ghent left several problems still to be resolved in respect to the border between the United States and the British North American colonies. Attempts to find solutions to these problems would be made during the ensuing years. The first problem, dealt with in 1817 by the Rush-Bagot Treaty, was the demilitarization of the Great Lakes and Lake Champlain. During the War of 1812, extensive ship-building races occurred on Lake Erie, Lake Ontario, and Lake Champlain. Naval battles on Lake Erie and Lake Champlain resulted in crucial victories for the United States and considerable damage to all the warships, but the opposing naval forces on Lake Ontario never actually met in battle, partially due to the reluctance of both Commodore Chauncey and British Admiral James Yeo.

During negotiations at Ghent, the British initially proposed that the Great Lakes remain in British control and that American forts on shore be dismantled. The American delegation refused this proposal, along with the one to establish an Indian nation between the Ohio River and Lake Erie. The status of the Great Lakes was not specifically mentioned in the Treaty of Ghent except that status of the lakes should remain as it was prior to the war. Many British and American naval armaments and forts would then still remain unless the problem was addressed in another treaty. The Rush-Bagot Treaty was signed in Washington, D.C. on April 18-19, 1817 by Acting United States Secretary of State Richard Rush and British Minister to the United States Sir Charles Bagot. This agreement to demilitarize the lakes showed that relations between the United States and Great Britain were improving. It was the first indication that the eventual border between the United States and Canada would not be armed

The following year more of the problems left unsolved by the Treaty of Ghent were addressed in London by an American delegation consisting of Albert Gallatin, who was ambassador to France at the time, and Richard Rush, the ambassador to Great Britain. The British negotiators were Frederick John Robinson, treasurer of the Royal Navy and member of the privy council, and Henry Goulburn, the undersecretary of state, who had been involved in negotiations for the Treaty of Ghent. Article I of the Treaty of 1818 secured fishing rights along Newfoundland and Labrador for the United States. Articles II and III directly related to the border between Canada and the United States.

The Treaty of Paris at the end of the American Revolution had placed the boundary between the United States and British North American possessions along a line going westward from the northwest corner of the Lake of the Woods to the Mississippi River. By 1818 further exploration had determined that the source of the Mississippi River was not as far north as the northwest corner of the Lake of the Woods and therefore the boundary was set along a line drawn from the most northwestern point of the Lake of the Woods due south to the 49th parallel and then along the 49th parallel of north latitude to the Rocky Mountains. This created the Northwest Angle, a small section of the present state of Minnesota that lies north of the 49th parallel and is accessible only through Canada.

The 49th parallel was apparently decided upon in order to designate a straight line boundary. The Louisiana Purchase from France by the United States in 1803 included the drainages of the Mississippi and Missouri Rivers which extended north of the 49th parallel into the future Canada province of Saskatchewan. On the other hand, the territory granted by Great Britain to the Hudson's Bay Company in 1670 included all the area draining into Hudson Bay. Since the Red River of the north drains into Hudson Bay, some of the land in the future states of Minnesota and North and South Dakota was originally part of Rupert's Land. In flat prairie country like this the actual watershed line was difficult to determine so the straight line of the 49th Parallel was a handy compromise. The choice of the 49th parallel turned out to be advantageous to the United States because the land drained by the upper Red River was considerably better adapted to farming than the arid land in southern Saskatchewan that became part of Canada.

The land that the United States obtained by designating the 49th parallel as the border was the southern part of the Selkirk Grant that Thomas Douglas, the fifth earl of Selkirk, obtained from the Hudson's Bay Company for a colonization project to relocate Scots that were made destitute by the social upheaval in Scotland after the introduction of sheep farming and the highland and lowland clearances. The Hudson's Bay Company hoped that the Red River settlement would provide food for its fur-trapping expeditions going into the northwest. The initial group of Scots arrived in 1812 and built Fort Douglas near the junction of the Red and Assiniboine rivers, but could not start farming until the following year. The Red River settlement was unfortunately located on the trails that both the North West Company and the Hudson's Bay Company fur-trapping parties used to reach their trading posts. The colony was soon embroiled in the bitter war between the fur companies, and was repeatedly attacked, abandoned, and then reestablished.

When the fur companies finally stopped fighting and combined under the name of the Hudson's Bay Company in 1821, the monopoly was legally strengthened and geographically expanded by Lord Bathurst. As a promised reward for the merger, Parliament passed an act on July 2, 1821 granting the Hudson's Bay Company control over the whole of British North America except for the colonies already occupying the Atlantic shore and the St. Lawrence-Lower Great Lakes area for an annual token payment of five shillings. Thus Great Britain turned over to the fur monopoly control of all British North America north of the 49th parallel from the Lake of the Woods to the Rocky Mountains. In addition, as specified in the Treaty of 1818, the land west of the Rocky Mountains between Russian American and Spanish America, known as the Oregon Territory, would be jointly controlled by the United States and Great Britain, which would be represented by the Hudson's Bay Company.

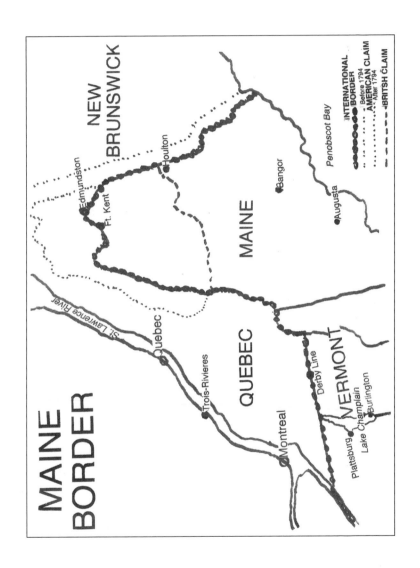

# Aroostook War

The Treaty of 1818 failed to resolve the problem of the Maine-New Brunswick border which resulted from the interpretation of the "highlands" referred to in the Treaty of Paris. The residents of Maine considered the highlands to be the watershed between rivers draining into the St. Lawrence River and those draining into the Atlantic ocean. The British, on the other hand, claimed that Mars Hill near the junction of the St. John and Aroostook rivers was the highlands referred to in the treaty and that the Aroostock River was the boundary. As Secretary of State in 1802, James Madison had confused the issue by defining the highlands as "elevated ground dividing the rivers falling into the Atlantic," which would be in line with the British claim. The disputed land was vital to Great Britain for two reasons. The tall pine trees in the Aroostook area were ideal for sailing vessel masts, which were necessary to the British navy after Napoleon signed a treaty with Russia that effectively closed the Baltic timber trade to Britain. Furthermore, the land north of the upper St. John River was a necessary military connection between the maritime provinces of New Brunswick and Nova Scotia and Lower Canada. The disputed land was valuable to Americans primarily for lumber.

Most of the settlers in the disputed region were French Canadians, who referred to themselves as Les Brayons, a term possibly relating to their origin in the Bray region of France. After the British forcefully removed Acadian farmers from the Bay of Fundy region in 1755 in the Grande Derangement, some of them moved north to land along the lower St. John River. They were displaced again in 1784 when Great Britain allotted land on the St. John River near Fredericton to Loyalists escaping the American Revolution. Crowded out of their new homes, some of the Acadian farmers petitioned the British governor of New Brunswick for land north of the great falls of the St. John River and settled in the fertile valley where the Madawaska River flows into the St. John. They were joined by more Acadians and Quebecois, and lived peacefully on farms along the rivers for more than thirty years.

John Baker, an American citizen, arrived in the disputed area around 1817 with his family. Initially he may have intended to become a British subject, but was persuaded by Maine land agents to pursue his rights as an American. He petitioned the state of Maine and received a land grant on the north side of the St. John River. Being a resident of the state of Maine wasn't enough for Baker. On the 4th of July in 1827, Baker and his family hoisted a homemade flag, showing an eagle beneath six red stars, and proclaimed the republic of Madawaska to be an independent American republic. They hired a French fiddler and some of the Brayons joined in the festivities. Several Americans signed a compact by which they agreed to adjust all disputes among themselves without appealing to British authority.

The New Brunswick provincial authorities objected to the Madawaska Flag and demanded its removal. When Baker refused, he was arrested and jailed in Fredericton. After the court fined Baker and sentenced him to the time already served in the Fredericton jail, he returned home. A stalemate ensued as land agents and census takers from both Maine and New Brunswick entered the disputed area only to be ignored or arrested. In the meantime, the negotiators appointed under the provisions of the Treaty of Ghent attempted to survey the area. When asked about the history of this survey, some current residents of Maine tell the story that Americans got the British so drunk that they followed the wrong river in the course of their surveying. Whether or not that actually happened, the negotiators failed to reach an agreement as to the boundary and the king of the Netherlands agreed to act as an arbitrator. His decision, rendered in January 1831, set the border at the St. John and St. Francis rivers rather than at the "highlands" referred to in the Treaty of Paris. This was an obvious attempt to compromise, taking into consideration the claims and interests of both sides.

On February 28, 1831, the Maine Legislature resolved not to accept the arbitration, contending that the king of the Netherlands was no longer a "neutral person of importance" since the Netherlands would be dependent on Great Britain after Belgium attained its independence. The Maine Legislature further recognized the town of Madawaska, consisting of an area three times larger than Rhode Island, and directed the inhabitants to organize a town government and send one representative to the Legislature. The residents of Madawaska organized a city government and elected Pierre Lizotte, one of the Brayons, to be their representative. Lizotte refused the position because he still considered himself a British subject. The Americans thought that the Brayons, who had been evicted from their homes twice by the British, would gladly become Americans. The Brayons, however, felt they would have a better chance to retain their language and culture under British rule. The United States government was willing to accept the compromise suggested by the king of the Netherlands, but finally agreed with the Maine Legislature that the federal government could not take land away from a sovereign state. The problem of the disputed territory was still not resolved.

Tensions increased in the winter of 1838-1839 when Canadian lumberjacks entered the Aroostook region to cut timber and then arrested a Maine land agent who was sent to expel them. Both Maine and New Brunswick called out their militias and the United States Congress, at the instigation of Maine, authorized a force of 50,000 soldiers and appropriated $10 million dollars to meet the emergency. The Bangor Rifle Corps members tendered their services to Major General Isaac Hodsdon and received orders on February 17 to meet at Bangor House equipped with rifles, ammunition, three days' rations, and blankets. They marched up the Houlton Road in bitter cold weather, arriving in Houlton on February 28. The Dexter Rifle Corps, one of the first militia groups to appear at Houlton, arrived in sartorial splendor, dressed in black velvet caps decorated with ostrich plumes, brownish-yellow coats faced and trimmed with black velvet, matching pantaloons with velvet stripes, knapsacks with black painted borders and the initials DRC in the middle. Their uniforms cost $30 each.

The New Brunswickers along the lower St. John River were descendants of Loyalists and feared that this Maine militia activity portended an American invasion of their province. The concern was not limited to New Brunswick. The Legislature of Nova Scotia voted a contingent of 10,000 men and money to aid New Brunswick in repelling the aggression of the state of Maine.

The armed militias of Maine and New Brunswick were facing each other across the St. John River when President Martin Van Buren called upon Major General Winfield Scott to take control. Scott had already received plaudits as a "diplomat general." He had evolved the technique of bringing a big stick and then speaking softly in dealing with Black Hawks in 1832 and the Seminole Indians in 1835. Early in 1838 he was sent to deal with Canadian insurgents on the Niagara peninsula during the *Caroline* affair, a border confrontation that threatened to result in war with Great Britain.

Some Americans living along the United States-Canada border, still hoping that Canada would eventually become part of the United States, were anxious to aid and abet any Canadians rebelling against British rule. A group of Canadian insurgents established a base on Navy Island in Canada territory on the Niagara River from which they planned to attack Upper Canada. American sympathizers brought them food and supplies utilizing the American-owned steamboat *Caroline*. Colonel Allan MacNab, commander of the Upper Canada militia, hoping to prevent the use of the *Caroline* as a supply ship, commissioned Commander Andrew Drew, R.N. to command a nocturnal expedition to destroy the *Caroline*. On December 29, 1837, Drew set out expecting to find the *Caroline* at Navy Island. He finally found it across the river moored at Schlosser, N.Y., and boarded the vessel. In the ensuing fight, one American was killed and the abandoned boat was set afire to drift towards Niagara Falls. There was great rejoicing in Upper and Lower Canada, and MacNab and Drew were presented swords in appreciation. American border communities activated militias anticipating an invasion from Canada.

On the evening of January 4, 1838, President Van Buren was hosting a political dinner at the White House with General Scott among the guests. Van Buren drew Henry Clay and Scott aside and whispered, "Blood has been shed." Then he turned to Scott and continued, "You must go with all speed to the Niagara frontier. The secretary of war is writing your instructions." Scott left the next morning and stopped in Albany to persuade Governor William Marcy to go with him in case they needed to use New York militia. On January 13 they visited Niagara Falls and made contact with Rensselaer Van Rensselaer, the leader of the group on Navy Island. Scott was able to persuade Van Rensselaer that the insurgents' cause was hopeless, and the group evacuated Navy Island. To prevent another similar incident, Scott outbid the insurgents who were trying to acquire another supply ship. As a local hero from the War of 1812, Scott was admirably suited for the task of persuading frontier Americans not to attempt further aggressive designs on Canada. Before he was again summoned to the United States-Canada border, Scott spent the remainder of 1838 supervising the Cherokee Nation on the Trail of Tears.

Scott arrived back at Washington D.C. on February 23, 1839 to find everyone alarmed about the prospect of war in Maine. Van Buren instructed Scott to do all he could to prevent war. Scott was not optimistic and replied, "Mr. President if you want war, I need only look on in silence. The Maine people will make it for you fast and hot enough. But if peace be your wish, I can give no assurance of success. The difficulties in the way will be formidable." Van Buren replied, "Peace with honor."

Scott had an ace in the hole in the form of his personal friendship with Major General John Harvey, the lieutenant governor of New Brunswick. The two soldiers faced each other several times on the Niagara frontier during the War of 1812. When Scott returned to duty after renouncing his pledge to remain neutral after he was taken prisoner in the Battle of Queenston, Harvey, the British adjutant, warned him that he would be treated harshly if captured again. They met again in 1813 at the Battle of Stony Creek where Harvey led the British forces that surprised Scott's army and saved the Niagara district for the British. Colonel Harvey's kindness to the American prisoners earned him the respect of the American army. Later that year, Scott was with Commodore Isaac Chauncey during the burning of York. Among the plunder that the American sailors were taking with them, Scott recognized a trunk with Harvey's name on it. Belongings in the trunk included a miniature painting of a beautiful young lady that Scott assumed to be Harvey's bride. Scott bought the painting from the sailor and returned it to Harvey. Scott is also reported to have saved Harvey's life when he was captured briefly while cut off from his reconnaissance party. A soldier was taking aim at Harvey when Scott knocked the rifle from his hand. Following the War of 1812, Scott and Harvey continued to correspond.

When Scott arrived at Augusta, Maine, in February 1839, he found a letter from Harvey dated January 13, 1839. "My Dear General," the letter began, "in a letter which doubtless failed to reach you, I assured you

General Winfield Scott

of the high degree of satisfaction which I had individually derived from hearing of your selection for the very delicate and difficult command on the frontier of the northern states opposite the British Provinces. From the high opinion I had formed of your character during the late war of

1813-1814, I felt that the circumstances of your nomination to that command involved the most satisfactory assurance of the sincerity of your General Government in their wish to preserve peace and friendship with England. My mind often reverts with great satisfaction to the interview in the Niagara Frontier and its immediate consequences. If the social history of those campaigns had been given to the world, you and I would stand crowned with the most glorious wreath which can encircle the head of a soldier, viz: that of having softened the savage character of warfare and faced it with the usages of civilized nations. I should rejoice in renewing my personal acquaintance with you ... Let that meeting be under my roof, in this House, and believe me you have no friend who could feel a higher degree of pleasure than myself in the opportunity of evincing towards you and yours the warm recollection which I retain of your friendly feelings and action towards me."

General Scott replied, prophetically, to Harvey on March 9, 1839 from army headquarters in Augusta: "How happy may we esteem ourselves, if a personal friendship commenced in the field and in opposite ranks can be made in any degree conducive to the preservation of peace between our countries for, if an immediate conflict of arms about the disputed territory can be avoided, to allow time to the two governments to adjust, at London or Washington, the great question in controversy, which I am persuaded may readily be done, I see no reason to apprehend another cause of serious misunderstanding between the two portions of the great Anglo-Saxon race for centuries to come. The ties of common blood, language, civil liberty, laws, customs, manners and interests must, in a reasonable period, that is as soon as we can forget past wars, and they are almost forgotten, work out a strong compact for reciprocal feelings far more binding than written engagements, which the other nations of the world would be wholly unable to dissolve or resist. Such a compact, although the two portions of the race are, and probably ever will remain under separate governments and of different forms, is necessary to both, in war as in peace, for who shall say what hostile combinations, in the next one hundred, seventy, or even thirty years may not take place among other nations to require the united strength of England and America for the safety of their common principles and interests?"

Scott went on to propose that, if he could get Harvey's assurance that the British forces would not attack the Maine militia and take military possession of the disputed area bordering the Aroostook River, he had no doubt but that the troops of Maine would be immediately recalled. However, he insisted that a small armed civil posse consisting of the land agent and sheriff be allowed to remain in the area to perform their civil duties. Harvey agreed to these conditions, stating that the British troops would restrict activity to the area north of the St. John River to maintain connection between New Brunswick and Lower Canada and to protect British subjects living in Madawaska

On March 12, Maine Governor John Fairfield indicated that, upon the assurance from Lieutenant Governor Harvey, he would abandon all idea of occupying the disputed area and the Maine militia would be withdrawn. Harvey produced the required assurance that the British would not occupy the disputed area and Scott assured Harvey that Governor Fairfield would make a similar declaration to the effect that it was not his intention to attempt to interrupt the usual communication between the provinces or to disturb New Brunswick in the possession of the Madawaska settlement. An uneasy armistice ensued. The only casualties of the Aroostook war were an American killed in a bar fight and numerous cases of frostbite.

Winfield Scott was again proclaimed a hero for preventing war with Britain, and feted by President Van Buren with a Washington banquet. His name started to be mentioned as a leading Whig candidate for president. Sir John Harvey did not fare as well. John Baker, the American who declared Madawaska to be an independent American republic, lived on the north side of the St. John River. He continued to have town meetings with other Americans and aided the American census taker in registering residents on the north side of the river. Harvey asked British Governor General Lord Sydenham if British troops should watch the area, but, fearing an armed conflict, did not want them to actually enter Madawaska. Sydenham, however, ordered the troops to be quartered at Madawaska and arrested John Baker again. At the end of December 1840, Sydenham complained to Colonial Secretary John Russell that Harvey was not consistent in his protection of British interests. On February 24, 1841 Harvey received a dispatch stating that the interests of Her Majesty's service required that he should not continue in the administration of the government of the Province of New Brunswick. This news was received with regret because Harvey's policies had made more friends than enemies.

The political climate on the northeast frontier was about to change because elections in both the United States and Great Britain placed men in charge that were more inclined to bring about a permanent solution to the border dispute.

# Webster/Ashburton Treaty

Lord Aberdeen became secretary of foreign affairs in Great Britain in 1841. He replaced Palmerston, who had foiled previous attempts to solve the Maine-New Brunswick boundary controversy in a way acceptable to the United States. Palmerston was a strong proponent for the British claim to the disputed territory. He replaced John Harvey, the lieutenant governor of New Brunswick who had negotiated with Winfield Scott to prevent the Aroostook War, because he felt that Harvey was too friendly to the Americans. Furthermore, he presented a map, presumably the result of a new boundary survey, that showed the same Aroostock River boundary that the British originally claimed.

The new Peel administration in London was anxious to improve relations with the United States and was acutely aware that there were several spots along the United States-Canada border that threatened to erupt in violence at any time. In addition to the Maine-New Brunswick border, there was a border conflict in the head waters of the Connecticut River that had led to the proclamation of the Independent Republic of Indian Stream in 1832. Along the Grand Portage west of Lake Superior the United States and Great Britain had conflicting claims. Eventually they would have to resolve the territorial boundaries of the Oregon Territory between the Spanish claim at thirty-two degrees north latitude and the Russian claim at fifty-four degrees- forty minutes north latitude. The Oregon Territory was still jointly occupied by the United States and Great Britain, as established by the Treaty of 1818. When this new British government received an indication that the United States was ready for new negotiations on the Maine-New Brunswick border, they designated Alexander Baring, Lord Ashburton, to be the British negotiator.

The United States also had a change in administration in 1841.

William Henry Harrison and John Tyler who had campaigned with the slogan "Tippicanoe and Tyler too" were elected in 1840. When Harrison died during the first year of his presidency, Tyler took over. The new secretary of state, Daniel Webster, who was more friendly to Great Britain than his predecessor, made the first move towards conciliation, because he felt that the conflict over the Maine-New Brunswick border would be the easiest to resolve. Webster realized that the most difficult part of the negotiation would be getting Maine to agree to any compromise that would allow Britain to control land for a military road connecting the Atlantic provinces and Quebec City. Webster realized that this particular land was more valuable to Britain than to the United States, and would be a good area to trade for more valuable land elsewhere.

In anticipation of the upcoming session of the Maine Legislature, Webster sent Jared Sparks, a distinguished historian and future president of Harvard, to Augusta to show the Maine Legislature a map that he had found in the French Foreign Office. This was a copy of the Mitchell map showing a red line corresponding to the British claim. Benjamin Franklin mentioned in his correspondence that, in December 1782, he had marked a Mitchell map such as this with a red line showing the proposed boundary. Sparks exhibited the map he had found, and, although it was not proven to be the same map that Franklin had marked with a red line, it produced the intended apprehension in Augusta. The Legislature decided that the compromise suggested by the king of the Netherlands might be the best that they could hope for.

Lord Ashburton arrived at Annapolis, Maryland, on April 1, 1842. He was well known in the United States, having been associated with the highest levels of Philadelphia society prior to departing to England in 1802. He had invested along with William Bingham in three million acres of land in the Kennebec and Penobscot areas of Maine. Ashburton was prepared with a list of areas to which Great Britain was willing to relinquish its claims in order to get the military road north of the St. John River. The United States was anxious to keep control of the northern end of Lake Champlain where they had built a fort costing a million dollars at Rouses Point. This became a problem when the forty-fifth parallel of north latitude was resurveyed after the Treaty of Ghent. The original survey, done by Valentine and Collins between 1771 and 1774, was found to be inaccurate, placing the forty-fifth parallel about five miles north of its true location. Fort Rouses, thereby, was actually north of the true forty-fifth parallel. Altogether about sixty-one square miles between the 1771 survey and the true forty-fifth parallel were disputed. Americans had settled and built homes in this area, and the British were not anxious to assimilate these Americans, feeling that they were not likely to become loyal British subjects. The British were also willing to agree to the American claim that Halls Stream, the westernmost branch, was the true source of the Connecticut River, thereby leaving the Connecticut Lakes in American territory. Another disputed area was along the Grand Portage between Lake Superior and Rainy Lake. Here, with no knowledge as to the potential value of the uninhabited land in question, the British would agree to split the disputed area. The triangular piece of land that the United States thus acquired turned out to be the site of the rich Masabi and Vermillion iron ore deposits. The British made further concessions regarding Sugar island in the St. Mary's River between Lake Huron and Lake Superior in order to get a border in northern Maine that would keep the Americans from controlling the highlands looking down on the St. Lawrence River.

The final description of the northern Maine border was as follows: "beginning at the monument at the source of the river St. Croix, as designated and agreed to by the commissioners under the fifth article of the treaty of 1794, between the governments of the United States and Great Britain, thence north, following the exploring line run and marked by the surveyors of the two governments in the years 1817 and 1818, under the fifth article of the Treaty of Ghent, to its intersection with the river St. John, and to the middle of the channel thereof; thence up the middle of the main channel of the said river St. John, to the mouth of the river St. Francis, thence up the middle of the channel of the said river St. Francis and of the lakes through which it flows, to the outlet of the Lake Pohenagamook; thence southwesterly, in a straight line to a point on the northwest branch of the river St. John, which point shall be ten miles distance from the main branch of the St. John, in a straight line, and in the nearest direction; but if the said point shall be found to be less than seven miles from the nearest point of the summit or crest of the highlands, that divide those rivers which empty themselves into the river St. Lawrence from those which fall into the river St. John, then the said point shall be made to recede down the said northwest branch of the river St. John to a point seven miles in a straight line, from the said summit or crest; thence, in a straight line, in a course about south eight degrees west, to a point where the parallel of latitude of 45 degrees 25 minutes north intersects the southwest branch of the St. John; thence, southerly by the said branch, to the source thereof

DANIEL WEBSTER.

in the highlands at the Metjarmette portage; thence, down the said highlands which divide the waters which empty themselves into the river St. Lawrence from those which fall into the Atlantic ocean, to the head of Hall's Stream; thence, down the middle of said stream, till the line thus run intersects the old line of boundary surveyed and marked by Valentine and Collins previously to the year 1774, as the 45th degree of north latitude, and which has been known and understood to be the line of actual division between the States of New York and Vermont on one side, and the British Province of Canada on the other; and, from said point of intersection, west, along the said dividing line as heretofore known and understood, to the Iroquois, or St. Lawrence river."

This complex negotiated boundary, rather than just following the St. John and St. Francis rivers as suggested by the king of the Netherlands, resulted in the loss of considerable area in the northwest to the state of Maine. Maine would have been better off had they agreed to the boundary suggested in 1831. After a 21 year struggle, the Webster-Ashburton Treaty, signed by President Tyler on November 10, 1842, conveyed to Great Britain from Maine 3,207,680 acres. Maine received half of the three million dollars awarded jointly to Maine and Massachusetts. The Madasaska region was cut in half by the St. John River. John Baker's land was in New Brunswick.

Neither Great Britain nor the United States were completely happy with the treaty. In Britain it was referred to the "Ashburton's Capitulation." Governor Fairfield of Maine stated that he was deeply disappointed in the terms, feeling that Maine had made a large concession in order in keep the peace. In 1933, a copy of Franklin's red line, traced on a 1775 Mitchell map for the Spanish government by its ambassador in France in 1782, was discovered in Madrid. It conformed perfectly to Maine's claim, as did Jay's copy of Mitchell's 1755 map, which was found after negotiations were concluded. Shortly after the treaty was signed, correspondence and vouchers relating to the boundary dispute were found in the State Department's secret archives. In 1846, the House Committee on Foreign Affairs brought charges against Daniel Webster for personally taking money from the president's secret service fund and using public money to corrupt the press in Maine. Webster was exonerated, and discontent with the Webster-Ashburton Treaty died down as other territorial considerations took central stage.

In Clay's cartoon Polk, urged on by the belligerent General Bunkum, faces English monarch Queen Victoria and Prince Albert across an ocean. In the distance, on "neutral Ground," Louis Philippe of France and Czar Nicholas I of Russia look on. Victoria (on her throne): "I've opened my Ports for the admission of your Corn, and I offer to settle the Oregon business by arbitration! What more can you expect? Beware how you rouse

to, I am willing to negotiate! General Bunkum, heavily armed and accompanied by a bald eagle: "I'm for war and the whole of Oregon, Kalifornia, Kanada, and Kuba; here's a bird that will cut your British lion's liver out, and eat it cold without sugar, by thunder!!!" On an island near Britain, Irish Repeal Movement leader Daniel O'Connell waves a "Repeal" club, threatening, "Give us repthe British Lion!" Prince Albert, in a heavy German accent: "I dink so doo!" Nearby (far left) the Duke of Wellington struggles to rouse the British lion, who says, "Unloose my chains and fill my belly! Then I'll fight." Polk, to Victoria: "You opened your ports to keep you from starvation! I offered to settle the Oregon question at 49 [degrees] and you refused—I won't arbitrate—I go the whole figure to 54 42 which, if you'll agree

ale, or the devil an Irishman will you get to join your ranks!" O'Connell also holds a bag of "rent," the term for American funds contributed in support of his movement. Czar Nicholas: "I shall have no objection to see John Bull get a good licking; It will help my Eastern views." Louis Philippe: "I got my fingers burnt by meddling in the Texas business, so I shall not interfere in this; especially as a war will bring grist to my mill!"

52

# Oregon Treaty

Lord Ashburton succeeded in most of his mission when the Webster-Ashburton Treaty settled the Maine-New Brunswick border, the Connecticut River source, the acceptance of the erroneous survey of the 45th parallel, and the division of the territory around of Grand Portage. However Secretary of State Webster and Ashburton decided not to undertake a settlement of the Oregon territory, which had been in joint possession of the United States and Great Britain since 1818. Neither the United States nor Great Britain felt sufficiently well prepared to resolve the Pacific boundary at the time, and they feared that the other accomplishments might be in jeopardy if the Webster-Ashburton treaty was not signed promptly while the Tyler administration still had leverage in the Senate. Furthermore, the oppressive Washington heat forced Ashburton to hurry the resolution of his primary objectives. At one point, he wrote Webster, "I must throw myself on your compassion to continue somehow or other to get me released. I continue to crawl about in this heat by day and to pass my nights in a sleepless fever. In short I shall positively not outlive this affair if it is to be much prolonged." A solution to the ownership of land west of the continental divide between the 42° and 54°40' parallels was again postponed, as it had been in 1827.

The British claim to the Oregon territory dated back to 1792 when Captain George Vancouver sailed up the Northwest coast of North America. He explored the Juan de Fuca Strait, and discovered and named the Gulf of Georgia, Puget Sound, and Port Discovery. He then continued on to Nootka Sound on the north end of Vancouver Island to conclude arrangements made between Spain and Great Britain in 1790 at the Nootka Sound Convention when Spain agreed to yield its exclusive claims and acknowledge British presence in the area. En route to Puget Sound, Vancouver encountered and conferred with Robert Gray, an American trader from Boston. Gray mentioned that he was going back to explore an area at 46-10 north latitude where he had observed river-colored water that might indicate the presence of a large river. Gray returned to that area and discovered the river which he named "Columbia" after his ship. This discovery of Gray's prompted the United States to claim sovereignty to land on the Pacific coast.

After Vancouver heard of Gray's discovery of the mouth of the Columbia River, he hurried back to investigate the area, finding the bar across the mouth of the river and its treacherous channel. Most of the other British exploration of the Pacific Northwest was accomplished by men in the pay of a group of Montreal fur traders organized as the North West Company. Alexander McKenzie crossed North America overland in 1793, reaching the Pacific Ocean near the mouth of the Bella Coola River, and discovered the Fraser River. Along with David Thompson and Duncan McGillivray, MacKenzie established a chain of trading posts in the northwest that included the upper reaches of the Columbia River.

Americans advanced their claims in the northwest in 1803 when President Thomas Jefferson sent Lewis and Clark to map the territory between St. Louis and the mouth of the Columbia River. When Thompson and McGillivray learned of the Lewis and Clark expedition, they renewed their efforts to control the area by exploring the upper Columbia and Fraser rivers and building trading posts in both the Fraser and Columbia basins. The Americans sought to compete with the North West Company for the fur trade. In 1811, German-born New York entrepreneur John Jacob Astor formed the Pacific Fur Company and established a settlement at the mouth of the Columbia River. When Thompson arrived at the mouth of the Columbia by an overland route, Astoria and the Americans were already there.

During the War of 1812, the British navy attempted to help the North West Company by sending a warship to the mouth of the Columbia River, but when the *HMS Raccoon* arrived, Captain William Black found that the North West Company had already bought Astoria from the American fur company for about fifty thousand dollars. Captain Black insisted that a ceremony be performed and the Union Jack hoisted over Astoria, renamed Fort George, even though it was already British. This ceremony was to cause complications in later negotiations because the Treaty of Ghent stipulated that all territory taken during the war should revert to its prewar status. For the next ten years, however, no Americans were in the Columbia River valley, and the British agents consolidated control of the fur trade. After further negotiations, the British did allow the Americans to reestablish their rights to Astoria, but Americans did not occupy it and the North West Company resumed control of the fort.

The Oregon Territory boundary was on the agenda for the 1818 negotiations. The British rejected an Americans suggestion of a division at the 49th parallel from the Lake of the Woods to the Pacific Ocean. The suggestion of the 49th parallel presumably dated from the 1713 Treaty of Utrecht under the assumption that it was the approximate boundary between British Rupert's Land and French Louisiana. The British and American negotiators did agree on the 49th parallel as the boundary from the Lake of the Woods as far as the Rocky Mountains, but the territory west of the mountains between the 42° and 54°40' parallels was allowed to remain open to citizens and subjects of both countries. Realizing that the North West Company was in a superior position to monopolize trade in the area, the Americans insisted that joint occupation be limited to ten years. John Quincy Adams attempted to strengthen American claims to the Oregon area in the Adams-Onis Treaty of 1819 by having Spain cede its claims to the Pacific Northwest north of the 42nd parallel to the Americans, even though Spain had presumably already relinquished these claims to the British at the Nootka Sound Convention. Russia, in 1824, relinquished claims to the Pacific Northwest below 54°40' north latitude, leaving Great Britain and the United States the only nations with claims in the area.

After rejecting the 49th parallel boundary to the coast, the British suggested that they would accept the 49th parallel to its intersection with the northeasternmost branch of the Columbia River and then the Columbia River to its mouth. The Americans, on the other hand, continued to insist that they would not concede any British presence south of the 49th parallel, even when the British offered an American enclave on the Olympic Peninsula. In 1827, the two nations finally agreed to continue joint use of the Oregon territory. This time, however, the Americans insisted that, rather than a fixed time limit for the joint occupation, either nation could give a year's notice that it wished to negotiate the boundary again. The British continued to insist upon control of the Columbia River because the North West Company agents argued that it was the critical entrance into the area.

In the meantime, the war between the North West Company and the Hudson's Bay Company was resolved by a merger in 1821. The resulting company retained the Hudson's Bay Company name, although many of the posts in the northwest continued to be manned by agents formerly with the North West Company. After the merger, Parliament granted the Hudson's Bay Company monopoly control over all of British North America, except for colonies already recognized on the Atlantic shore and in the St. Lawrence/Lower Great Lakes area, for the yearly payment of five shillings, renewable in twenty-one years. The Hudson's Bay Company, therefore, was granted control of the Pacific Northwest, even though it was not originally part of Rupert's Land.

Governor George Simpson, the bastard son of a Scottish merchant, ruled the Hudson's Bay Company for the next four decades, ably assisted in its Columbia Department by three former North West Company agents, Dr. John McLoughlin, Peter Skene Ogden, and James Douglas. After the merger, the Hudson's Bay Company was reluctant to keep the half-dozen posts south of the 49th parallel that it inherited from the North West Company because they were expensive to maintain and not very profitable. Simpson was ordered to survey the district, cut expenses and reorganize the trade. When he arrived at Astoria in November 1824, accompanied by Dr. John McLoughlin, his designated commander of the Columbia Department, he found that the fort was being run in an extravagant and self-indulgent manner. Therefore, he cut the staff in half and ordered that Company headquarters be moved about a hundred miles inland to the Columbia River's north shore six miles past the mouth of the Willamette River. On March 19, 1825, they raised the Union Jack and formally named the new headquarters Fort Vancouver. During his visit, Simpson devised a plan to keep the American mountain men at bay south of the Columbia River. He left instructions that the area was to be trapped bare of every last beaver so that there would be little incentive for American trappers to occupy it. Simpson appointed Peter Skene Ogden to head up this methodical destruction of animal life.

McLoughlin, a former North West Company doctor, continued to be the trader in charge of the Hudson's Bay Company Columbia Department for the next twenty-two years. He ruled Fort Vancouver with such benevolent authority that he has been called the "Father of Oregon." In addition to the fur trade, he set up sawmills and flour mills and established large farming and fishing operations manned by servants living in a village outside the fort. Every evening traders and guests gathered at the Fort Vancouver officers mess, presided over by McLoughlin, with fare including roast beef and pork, baked salmon, and farm-raised vegetables served on blue earthenware dishes. While the Hudson's Bay Company presence served as a deterrent to American territorial aspirations, it provided the only available support system for mountain men and would-be settlers. Acting against the orders of his superiors, who saw no good reason to help potential enemies, McLoughlin not only welcomed all comers but granted them supplies on extended credit terms, thus encouraging settlement and strengthening American claims to the Oregon country. Reports of successful farming ventures at Fort Vancouver prompted independent American backers to organize expeditions into the area.

McLoughlin's main adversaries were his Hudson's Bay Company superiors. His generous treatment of American settlers and his diversification into non-fur related enterprises aroused the antagonism of George Simpson, who regarded himself primarily as an efficient colonial administrator. McLoughlin, on the other hand, felt that he was helping to found a new society. Within a decade of Fort Vancouver's founding, both the Missouri Fur Company and the Rocky Mountain Fur Company, the Hudson's Bay Company's main rivals, were bankrupt. The Snake River basin had been swept clean of both beaver and mountain men.

While McLoughlin chose to control the fur trade by establishing permanent inland posts, Governor Simpson insisted on expanding a fleet of trading ships. The rift between Simpson and McLoughlin deepened over the years as McLoughlin was forced to take care of the crews of the trading boats. On a trip up the northwest coast in 1841, Simpson was impressed with the excellent harbor on the southern tip of Vancouver Island. When he returned, he ordered McLoughlin to dismantle most of the northern trading posts, because trade would be conducted from the decks of the ship *Beaver* instead. Shortly thereafter, the headquarters of the Columbia Department was moved from Fort Vancouver to a new fort on Vancouver Island.

Postponement of a resolution to the Oregon boundary dispute during negotiations for the Webster-Ashburton Treaty caused a situation to develop that threatened to result in war between the United States and Great Britain. Word of the beauty of the Oregon country was spreading throughout America. The year 1843 opened a new era in Oregon migration. Great cavalcades of settlers replaced the small trains of former years, and they petitioned Congress to take action to counteract British encroachment in the Oregon territory. Two hundred wagons left Westport, Missouri, launching the "Great Migration" of 1843. John Calhoun, who succeeded Webster as Secretary of State in the Tyler administration, adopted the strategy of masterly inactivity, assuming that the settlers occupying the Oregon territory would cement American claims to the region south of the 49th parallel. The concept of "Manifest Destiny" was inflaming the United States. Democrat James Polk campaigned for president in 1844 with the slogan "Fifty-four Forty or Fight." Polk was serving notice that, if elected, his administration would press the United States claim to all the Oregon territory south of Russian America.

Masterly inactivity was catching the British unaware. If they wanted to preserve their position in Oregon, they would either have to negotiate or undertake some action to balance the increased pressure of American settlement. Both governments were anxious to meet and negotiate before the Polk administration could take control, but they were undecided whether negotiations should take place in Washington or in London. British Foreign Secretary Lord Aberdeen gave Richard Pakenham full powers to negotiate the Oregon dispute in Washington, while the Tyler administration instructed United States Minister to Britain Edward Everett to deal with the Peel administration in London.

Pakenham left London at the end of 1843 with instructions from Aberdeen to renew the 1826 boundary proposal of the 49th parallel as the boundary as far as its intersection with the Columbia River and then the Columbia to its mouth. The British proposal included an enclave for the Americans on the Olympic Peninsula. Pakenham's optimism about getting the Americans to settle the Oregon question dimmed because the United States administration was absorbed in negotiating the annexation of Texas. On February 3, 1845, the House passed the Oregon Bill which allowed for the organization of territorial government in Oregon and the establishment of forts along the Oregon trail. An amendment to the Oregon Bill stated that the United States was serving notice to Great Britain that it intended to abrogate the 1827 agreement for joint occupation. Negotiations were still stalled when James Polk, the expansionist Democrat, assumed the presidency on March 4, 1845.

In his inaugural address, Polk satisfied the crowd with remarks about expansionism. Since the Tyler administration had finally succeeded in authorizing the annexation of Texas, Polk's plans for expansion turned to Oregon. Pakenham reported to London that the Senate session ended with no decision on the Oregon Bill. At his initial meeting with James Buchanan, the new secretary of state, Pakenham raised the possibility of arbitration on the boundary. Buchanan indicated that he intended to approach the Oregon question on the principle of give and take. Pakenham speculated that Buchanan planned to propose a 49th parallel boundary, leaving Vancouver Island and free navigation on the Columbia River to the British, and he believed that such a proposal could only succeed if presented by the Americans. If Great Britain made the proposal, the Americans would probably refuse it.

On July 16, Buchanan and Pakenham resumed negotiations and Buchanan presented the American proposal. He began with an exaggerated recital of the basis for American rights to the area as far north as Russian America, and then presented a compromise of the 49th parallel with British rights to ports on Vancouver Island, but with no mention of free navigation on the Columbia River. At the same time Buchanan briefed Louis McLane, the new United States minister to Great Britain, on how he should present the United States offer to the Peel administration in London. In Washington, Pakenham, who had conflicting instructions on how he should react to the American offer, immediately rejected it. Perhaps Polk anticipated a refusal to his offer so that he could pursue continued efforts to claim the entire Oregon territory. When McLane prepared to resume negotiations in London, he received word that President Polk had withdrawn his compromise offer. Pakenham had neglected to present the American proposal with a counter offer and had not consulted with his superiors in London before rejecting the American offer. Aberdeen chastised Pakenham and advised him to rescind his rejection in the hope that Buchanan would cancel the withdrawal of the American offer. If this failed, Pakenham should again fall back on the suggestion of arbitration.

At this point, negotiations were stalemated. President Polk refused to submit his offer again. Aberdeen suggested arbitration, but the Americans refused on the basis that an unbiased arbitrator would be difficult to find. Both the Polk and Peel administrations had constituencies that required the upholding of intangibles like national honor for the British and manifest destiny for the Americans. The actual territory involved was a secondary consideration. Some Americans, such as Senator Thomas Hart Benton and veteran diplomat, Albert Gallatin, admitted that the American claims to area north of the 49th parallel were on shaky grounds. McLane was surprised that Aberdeen was so insistent on Columbia River navigation rights because the river was barely navigable and the Hudson's Bay Company had abandoned Ft. Vancouver. Navigation on the Columbia had become Aberdeen's issue through which to preserve national honor.

In the meantime, both Great Britain and the United States were preparing for conflict. The British cabinet allocated a thousand pounds to Simpson for defense and the British navy moved ships in and out of Oregon waters. McLane reported from London that the British were rearming. Trouble with Mexico was brewing for the Americans, making a prompt settlement on the Oregon boundary a priority. Buchanan succeeded in getting Polk to agree to submit any British offer to the Senate for advise and consent. There was good evidence that the Senate would agree to a 49th parallel boundary so that Polk could blame the Senate for the compromise. McLane was still worried that the Americans would not agree to navigation rights on the Columbia, so Aberdeen agreed that these rights should be limited to use by the Hudson's Bay Company. The Americans agreed because the navigation rights would only apply as long as the Hudson's Bay Company continued to hold the British contract in the area and therefore would not be perpetual.

By the time that Buchanan and Pakenham signed the Oregon Treaty in June 1846, the United States was at war with Mexico. The agreement provided for the extension of the existing boundary between the United States and British North America westward along the 49th parallel to the middle of the channel separating Vancouver Island from the mainland. From there the line would continue through the center of the Juan de Fuca Strait to the Pacific Ocean. In addition, the United States promised to guarantee to the Hudson's Bay Company and other affected British subjects navigation of the Columbia, portage rights along the river, and property rights south of the 49th parallel. When news of the treaty reached Oregon in November, it was greeted with excitement and relief, not with disappointment at forfeiture of territory north of the 49th parallel.

The Oregon Treaty, signed on June 15, 1846, salvaged for the Hudson's Bay Company the mainland territory north of the 49th parallel and Vancouver Island. The Company did not immediately abandon its Oregon-based operations. The last of its American trading posts was closed in 1871. Legal proceedings to compensate the Hudson's Bay Company for its original rights of possession dragged on for most of the next decade. The United States government eventually paid the Company $650,000, including $200,000 for the agricultural lands on Puget Sound.

Dr. John McLoughlin did not fare as well. The London Committee terminated his superintendency of the Columbia Department and demoted him. Deeply offended by their treatment of him, McLoughlin resigned. He retired to Oregon City on the Willamette River and applied for United States citizenship. Suspicious because he was British, a Catholic, and a former Bay man, the settlers whom he had helped turned on him and arranged to have his property confiscated. In addition, Simpson insisted that McLoughlin pay back, out of his own pocket, the outstanding balances for the goods he had sold on credit to help incoming settlers, who refused to honor their debits because they claimed their former benefactor was a traitor. The "Father of Oregon" died on September 1, 1857, bitterly indignant to the end.

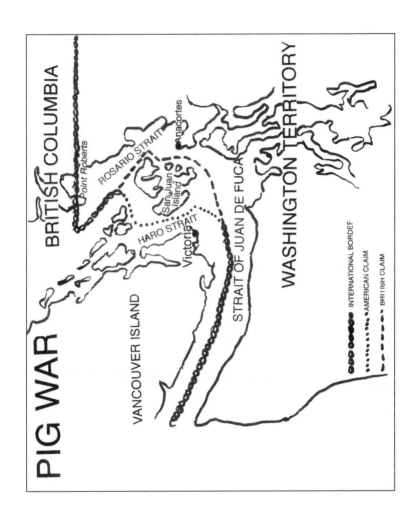

PIG WAR

BRITISH COLUMBIA

Point Roberts

ROSARIO STRAIT

Anacortes

San Juan Island

HARO STRAIT

Victoria

STRAIT OF JUAN DE FUCA

WASHINGTON TERRITORY

VANCOUVER ISLAND

INTERNATIONAL BORDER
AMERICAN CLAIM
BRITISH CLAIM

# Pig War

Both Great Britain and the United States wished to conclude the Oregon Treaty negotiations before the British government was due to change in June 1846 with Lord Palmerston becoming Foreign Minister again. Palmerston was known to be more rigid in his foreign policy toward the United States. The United States was anxious to resolve the Oregon border so it could concentrate on the war with Mexico. Although several men were aware of an ambiguity in the language of the Oregon Treaty that, unless resolved, would result in future conflict between the two nations, the problem was not addressed prior to signing the Treaty. The Treaty stated that the boundary should be continued along the forty-ninth parallel to the middle of the channel which separates the continent from Vancouver Island and thence southerly through the middle of the channel and the Juan de Fuca Straits to the Pacific Ocean.

Hudson's Bay Company officials knew that there actually were at least two channels cutting south through the Gulf of Georgia. After reviewing a draft of the treaty, Sir John Pelly, governor of the Hudson's Bay Company, pointed this out to Lord Aberdeen in London, and presented him with a map on which "Canal de Arro" between San Juan Island and Vancouver Island was identified, but the channel that was red-lined as "Vancouver's track" was Rosario Strait which passes between the San Juan Island group and the continental United States. United States Secretary of State James Buchanan also expressed alarm in a June 6 letter to Louis McLane, the American minister in London, that Article 1 of the Treaty did not specify Canal do Arro (Haro) as the appropriate channel through the Gulf of Georgia. In their hurry to conclude the Oregon Treaty negotiations, both the United States and Great Britain ignored Buchanan's observation and Pelly's protest and signed the Treaty on June 15. Both nations promptly ratified the Treaty without resolving the ambiguity about the channel passing through the San Juan Islands.

Hudson's Bay Company Governor George Simpson went to Washington in February 1847 to suggest that a commission be appointed to resolve the issue of sovereignty in the San Juan Islands since British survey ships were further studying the geography of the area. The San Juan Islands may have been unimportant specks on the world map to the foreign office in London, but to James Douglas, the Hudson's Bay Company's chief factor in the New Caledonia district and Vancouver Island governor, the San Juan Islands were of great importance. As far as he was concerned, they were all definitely owned by Great Britain and part of his territory.

Douglas, the illegitimate mulatto son of a Glasgow merchant who owned sugar estates in British Guiana, was educated in England and joined the North West Company as a teenager in 1819. When the North West Company joined the Hudson's Bay Company in 1824, he was assigned to Fort St. James in the New Caledonia Department. Douglas was transferred to Fort Vancouver in 1830, where he became chief factor in 1839, and then replaced John McLoughlin who retired in 1846. He was involved in choosing the site for a fort on Vancouver Island in 1842 and took over Fort Victoria in 1849 when it replaced Fort Vancouver as headquarters of the New Caledonia Department.

In that same year, while the discovery of gold was bringing scores of prospectors to California, Great Britain granted Vancouver Island to the Hudson's Bay Company for the token yearly rent of seven shillings. One proviso in the grant was that the Hudson's Bay Company must establish a settlement of colonists on the island within five years or lose the grant. Settlement had never before been a prime interest of the fur company because settlers were a hindrance to the fur trade. Vancouver Island was a long way from England and the incentives offered were not adequate to entice many potential settlers. Most of the original settlers turned out to be retired employees of the Hudson's Bay Company.

Richard Blanshard, a young British barrister, accepted the position of governor of the Colony of Vancouver Island, but he resigned after a year, finding it too difficult to adapt to the rigors of colonial life. Douglas then accepted the governorship and was also appointed vice admiral of the British navy for Vancouver Island while continuing to be chief factor for the Hudson's Bay Company. Douglas thus became the primary representative of the British empire in the northwest with legal and military responsibilities.

As the lucrative fur trade decreased when silk replaced beaver in men's top hats, the Hudson's Bay Company diversified into fishing and farming. The Puget Sound Agricultural Company, a Hudson's Bay subsidiary, which supplied the Russian American Company in Sitka with food, was also one of Douglas' responsibilities. While he was at Fort Vancouver, Douglas witnessed the influx of American settlers into the Oregon territory. He didn't want this to happen in other territory that he considered British, including the San Juan Islands. Since San Juan Island, only seven miles from Vancouver Island, had treeless land that was well suited for ranching, the Puget Sound Agricultural Company established a sheep ranch on the island's southern end.

On December 15, 1853, a group of Hawaiian herdsmen, led by Chief Agent Charles Griffin turned 1350 sheep loose to graze on a sweeping prairie overlooking the Strait of Juan de Fuca. Griffin also brought seed for crops and other farm animals, including several Berkshire boars. He called the main station Belle Vue Farm and established sheep stations at several other places on the island.

Isaac Neff Ebey, the American customs collector for the area, considered San Juan Island American territory and presented Griffin a duty bill, stating that the sheep would be liable for seizure unless it was paid. Rather than pay the duty, Griffin hoisted the Union Jack over Belle Vue Farm. Ebey then appointed Henry Webber assistant customs collector, placing him in a cabin next to Belle Vue Farm with an American flag prominently displayed. Douglas countered by sending British Customs Collector James Sangster to the island and attempting to arrest Webber, who resisted with a brace of pistols and a knife. Rather than force the issue, Douglas instructed Griffin to leave Webber alone unless he interfered with British property. Ebey instructed Webber to keep track of the sheep, but not to attempt to collect duty. Webber and Griffin lived side by side and soon become fast friends.

While peace reigned on San Juan Island, correspondence continued between American and British officials indicating that a commission would soon meet to decide the boundary. United States Secretary of State William Marcy sent a semi-apologetic letter to Douglas, stating that the Americans had no reason to collect customs duty from the

Hudson's Bay Company or interfere with their operations while the ownership of the islands was disputed. In early 1855, raids by northern Indians drove the Americans, including Webber, from San Juan Island, but both the United States and Great Britain continued to claim ownership of the islands. An American revenue cutter continued to watch San Juan Island and officials of Whatcom County in Washington Territory still threatened to collect local taxes on Belle Vue Farm.

Starting in October 1854, Whatcom County Sheriff Ellis Barnes ordered Griffin to pay $80.53 in back taxes or face a sheriff's sale. No bidders appeared at Barnes' first attempt to hold a sheriff's sale, but, on March 30, 1855, an armed party of Whatcom County officials arrived after dark, rounded up sheep in a makeshift pen, and conducted a starlight auction. This time more than forty breeding rams were sold, but the Americans did not have adequate boats to carry them to the mainland. While attempting to load the rams into canoes, some butted the deputies and ran away. The Americans got away with 34 breeding rams, with Griffin and several herdsmen in pursuit.

Douglas had British Ambassador John Crampton in Washington, D.C. make a claim on the United States for the rams. Although Washington Territorial Governor Isaac Stevens did not approve of the sheep auction, he felt obliged to support the Americans. Secretary of State Marcy again played the peacemaker by sending a letter instructing Stevens to "abstain from all acts, on the disputed grounds, which are calculated to provoke any conflict." Marcy went on to indicate that "the title ought to be settled before either party should attempt to exclude the other by force." For the next several years, copies of this Marcy letter were carried by every British official in the northwest to use against any overreaching Yankee.

The sheep incident prompted the United States Congress to move on appropriating money to pay for a boundary commission, which the British had proposed back in 1848. When the money was allocated on August 11, 1856, Archibald Campbell was appointed commissioner, with an astronomer and surveyor to assist him in marking the boundary between the Rocky Mountains and the Pacific. The British commissioner Captain James Prevost was given secret instructions to press for Rosario Strait and also for an adjustment on Point Roberts, a small peninsula of land that dips below the 49th parallel from the British Columbia mainland into United States territory. The most important objective for the British was to continue possession of Vancouver Island. Prevost believed that San Juan Island was important to form a wall of defense protecting Vancouver Island and the Royal Navy anchorage at Esquimalt. Campbell's instructions from Secretary of State Marcy were just as partisan as those of the British.

The British and American commissioners met six times between June and September 1857 but failed to reach an agreement. In November, Prevost proposed that they agree on a Middle Channel that would award San Juan Island to the British and the rest of the island group to the United States, but Campbell refused this alternative. From then on the commissioners seemed to avoid each other and the status of the San Juan Islands remained unresolved.

Americans still feared the northern Indians, and no settlers appeared on San Juan Island until some frustrated miners began drifting over there in the summer of 1858. Lyman Cutlar, a failed miner from Kentucky, arrived on San Juan Island in April 1859 with his Indian wife and child and squatted on land that Belle Vue Farm was using for a sheep run. Cutler had a potato patch, partially enclosed by a three-sided fence that was not adequate to keep out livestock. He claimed to have repeatedly driven Griffin's black boar out of his potato patch, and that Belle Vue Farm was aware of the problem. On June 15, 1859, his patience ran out and he shot the hog. Cutlar went to Griffin and offered to pay for the hog, but refused to pay the $100 that Griffin claimed the hog was worth.

Accounts differ as to what happened next. Three men from Vancouver Island came to San Juan Island in the Hudson's Bay Company's trading ship *Beaver* and met with Cutlar. Alexander Grant Dallas, a Hudson's Bay official and Douglas' son-in-law, may have threatened Cutlar, although he later denied it. Following this meeting, the American settlers consolidated to support Cutlar. Deputy Collector of Customs Paul K. Hubbs, Jr., the leader of the Americans, organized an old-fashioned Fourth of July flag-raising celebration to demonstrate their solidarity and opposition to the British. The former miners were bitter about the treatment they had encountered in the upper Fraser River gold diggings, because claims on British land were reserved for the crown and Douglas forced them to pay monthly fees. They raised the American flag on a 45-foot pole in front of Hubbs' log cabin, which was about 100 yards above Belle Vue Farm. Griffin promptly raised the Union Jack over his cabin.

Brigadier General William Selby Harney, the military commander of the Department of Oregon, visited San Juan Island on July 9, 1859 during his regular inspection tour of his territory. Harney had distinguished himself with bravery during the Mexican War, but was known to be impetuous and, occasionally, to fail to follow orders. The pre-Civil War army was full of political factionalism. Harney, a Democrat like his patron, Andrew Jackson, harbored resentment toward Whig generals like Winfield Scott. Harney, also shared Jackson's hatred of the British. In spite of his aversion toward the Hudson's Bay Company, Harney had paid a courtesy call on Douglas just before the San Juan Island visit. During this meeting, there was no mention of the pig incident.

General Harney took special notice of Hubbs' American flag as he entered Griffin Bay. After Harney landed, Hubbs approached the general and related at length details of the pig shooting and the harassment of Cutlar by the Hudson's Bay Company. Two days after Harney's visit, Hubbs submitted a petition to Harney, signed by twenty-two American settlers, including Lyman Cutlar, asking for military protection against the northern Indians. This petition actually commended the British for helping American settlers in time of need.

Upon his return to headquarters at Fort Vancouver, Harney dispatched Special Orders No. 72, directing Captain George E. Pickett to leave Fort Bellingham and occupy San Juan Island. The following day he wrote Lieutenant General Winfield Scott at the War Department a letter to accompany the petition explaining his action. In the letter he invoked Manifest Destiny and claimed that the British would never succeed in colonizing Vancouver Island. Despite the petition's emphasis on northern Indians, Harney made little mention of them in his letter, and dwelled instead on the pig incident, the harassment of Cutlar, and the "oppressive interference of the authorities of the Hudson's Bay Company at Victoria...." Harney also claimed that Hudson's Bay officials had arrived in a British warship rather than on the *Beaver*. Several interesting speculations have been advanced as to why Harney chose Pickett for this mission. General George McClellan, a classmate of Pickett's at West Point, theorized that the two Southerners conspired to start a war with Great Britain to unite the North and South in a common cause and, thereby, prevent the Civil War.

On July 26, 1859, the USS *Massachusetts* landed Captain Pickett and his Company at Griffin Bay on San Juan Island. Pickett was ordered to find a suitable site for four to six companies, preferably in a defensible location. However, he ordered his tents pitched on about 300 square yards of open hillside above the Hudson's Bay Company dock. While the tents were going up, he ordered the following proclamation to be posted: "This being United States territory, no laws other than those of the United States, nor courts, except such as are held by virtue of said laws, will be recognized or allowed on this island."

Douglas, in his capacity as acting vice-admiral in the absence of Rear Admiral R. Lambert Baynes, ordered Captain Michael De Courcy, to dispatch a warship to San Juan Island. The 31-gun steam frigate MHS *Tribune*, under the command of Captain Geoffrey Phipps Hornby, arrived at San Juan Island on the evening of July 29,1859, Hornby's orders were to prevent the landing of more United States soldiers. Hornby's initial report to DeCourcy indicated that the American force consisted of about 50 soldiers with two howitzers and an equal number of armed civilians. A.G. Dallas, who was on board the *Tribune*, advised Douglas to dispatch another ship to support Hornby, and Douglas ordered DeCourcy to send the steam frigate MHS *Plyades* to San Juan Island. At this point the Royal Navy balked. After receiving reports from Hornby and British Border Commissioner Captain James Prevost of the MHS *Satellite*, DeCourcy realized that the situation was becoming dangerous, and, even though Douglas was nominally in charge, he would have to answer to Admiral Baynes. In a face-to-face discussion with Douglas, the captains expressed reservations about the deployment of British ships against United States troops. They advised that attempts to arrest Pickett should be abandoned, but that a detachment of marines could be held ready in case needed. In the meantime, Prevost, after sending orders to Hornby not to interfere with the Americans, left for Semiahmoo, attempting, unsuccessfully, to confer with Archibald Campbell, his counterpart on the border commission.

San Juan Island was becoming a center of activity. Visitors and newspaper reporters were pressing Pickett for interviews. The harbor was already full of ships, both British and American naval vessels, as well as merchant ships, when the USS *Massachusetts* arrived with Company I, Fourth Infantry on board to reinforce Pickett's troops. However, Hornby reported to Douglas that even though United States troops arrived in the harbor on August 1, they left the same day without landing rather than confronting the British warships.

The events of August 1 irritated James Douglas. First the Royal Navy captains refused to accept his orders, and then his own Vancouver Island council urged him not to place royal Marines on the island. As the Hudson's Bay Company agent for Great Britain in the Pacific Northwest he had suffered the indignity of having to give up British sovereignty south of the 49th parallel. He had founded the Vancouver Island colony, of which he considered the San Juan Islands a part. He had also acted decisively to save New Caledonia, now called British Columbia, from the Americans during the Fraser River gold rush. Douglas, the agent of a commercial enterprise, was the leading advocate for British "manifest destiny" in North America. He decided not to sit back and be overrun again by the Yankees. If Pickett's soldiers remained, he would ignore the British Navy, land an equal number of marines to counterbalance Pickett, and declare joint military law on the island.

Hornby, who received Douglas' orders to land the British marines, was, at the time, the highest ranking British naval officer in the area. DeCourcy was on the way to San Francisco with Lt. Colonel John S. Hawkins of the Royal Marines, who was being dispatched to inform the British government in London about the situation on San Juan Island. Boundary Commissioner Prevost was still trying to find his American counterpart Archibald Campbell. On August 2, forty-six marines and fifteen Royal engineers arrived at Griffin Bay. Hornby arranged a meeting with Pickett and proposed joint military occupations. Pickett insisted that he needed the consent of Harney before considering this proposal. Hornby then produced his copy of the Marcy letter and showed it to Pickett, who had never seen it. Suspecting that Pickett's orders had not come from Washington, Hornby decided to keep the marines on board ship and wait for the return of Admiral Baynes.

Baynes, who was in his sixties, had seen service as a midshipman in the War of 1812. His cool demeanor was a contrast to the aggressive behavior of Harney and Douglas, and he did not tolerate foolish behavior. When Baynes arrived at Esquimalt, he commended Hornby for avoiding a potentially disastrous situation by refusing to land the marines. He formally cancelled Douglas' order and directed Hornby to avoid interfering with Pickett.

With a military confrontation prevented, for the moment at least, civilian activity thrived. San Juan Village was being built with buildings from abandoned mining camps on Bellingham Bay. Liquor establishments opened and young Indian women arrived. Soldiers, sailors, and marines were ready and willing to participate, and reporters from Victoria were there to describe the activity. However, the danger was not over.

When General Harney received Pickett's letter describing his encounter with Hornby, he pictured the menacing British warships in the harbor and decided that Pickett needed support. The following day, he wrote the War Department that he was sending Lt. Colonel Silas Casey to San Juan Island with reinforcements consisting of three more companies with heavy guns. Casey's orders were to reinforce Pickett and take commend on San Juan Island. To impress the British, Casey was to remove the *Massachusetts's* eight 32-pound naval guns and place them in position to protect the harbor. Since Pickett was apprehensive about the British reaction to the landing of reinforcements, Casey asked Hornby for a meeting. Several hours later, Hornby came ashore with Prevost and Campbell, the border commissioners. When Casey asked Hornby from whom he received his orders, Hornby responded, "Admiral Baynes." Casey decided to go to Esquimalt Harbor to confer with Admiral Baynes

Changing into dress uniforms, complete with plumes and epaulets, Casey and Pickett, along with Campbell, proceeded to Victoria the next morning, but the meeting fell through because of protocol. Casey insisted that Baynes leave his flagship to meet on the *Shubrick*, the lighthouse tender that had brought the Americans to Victoria. Baynes had shown forbearance by not actively challenging the American invasion of disputed territory, but he refused to descend to meeting a lesser-ranking officer on a much smaller boat. For several hours they haggled over a place for the meeting with Pickett serving as messenger boy. Casey finally gave up and returned to San Juan Island.

Casey reported to Harney about the failed meeting. The chilly response he had received from the Royal Navy spurred him to ask for four more companies of soldiers and a detachment of engineers to build fortifications, which Harney of course approved. Douglas was also unhappy, primarily because Casey had requested to meet with Baynes rather than with him, so he wrote to Colonial Secretary Lord Lytton in London stressing that the Americans had established military occupation of San Juan Island apparently without the authority of the United States Government. Commissioner Archibald Campbell finally joined in the protests, complaining to Harney that he had not been informed that Pickett's landing would be more extensive than an exercise to chase Indians.

On San Juan Island, two large warships were aiming guns at Casey and his troops while they built earthworks for their heavy guns. Hornby was alarmed, but Baynes continued to insist that British warships do everything in their power to avoid a confrontation with United States troops. In the meantime, civil officers of the two countries acted jointly in banning the sale of liquor on the island. Guests continued to arrive, including both the new and the former governors of Washington Territory, who watched nine American companies parade in review led by Colonel Casey on horseback. Not to be outdone, the British invited the new governor to have tea and watch gun drills on board the MHS *Satellite*. Governor Douglas and General Harney continued to correspond. Douglas showed Harney the Marcy letter, which Harney claimed never to have seen, and Harney accused the Hudson's Bay Company of inciting Indians to attack American settlers, as the British had done in the War of 1812.

While Harney and Douglas were accusing each other, officials in Washington and London finally learned about the confrontation on San Juan Island. In the mid-nineteenth century, telegraph had yet to span the continent and travel between the coasts passed through the Panama isthmus on a railroad just completed in 1855. Harney's July 19 dispatch finally reached Lieutenant General Winfield Scott and President Buchanan on September 3, 1859. Buchanan was one of the negotiators who had pointed out the ambiguity in the Oregon Treaty concerning the ownership of the San Juan Islands. He was also aware of Harney's thrust into Mexico without orders early in the Mexican War and his insubordination to General Scott. He realized the danger of an armed conflict with Great Britain when the United States was itself on the brink of a civil war.

British Foreign Secretary Lord John Russell learned of Pickett's landing by telegram from Ambassador Lord Lyons. Russell proposed the Middle Channel as a reasonable compromise, as previously suggested by boundary commissioner Prevost, insisting that the British should at least keep San Juan Island. As the danger of conflict increased, a resolution of the water boundary was essential.

When Harney's August 7 dispatch declaring that Casey had landed with reinforcements reached Buchanan, he turned again to Winfield Scott, who had successfully forestalled armed conflicts with Great

Britain in 1837 on the Niagara border following the *Caroline* affair and in Maine in 1839 during the Aroostock War. Buchanan notified Scott by telegram on September 14, stressing that the general was to focus on immediate peace, leaving the boundary specifics to the commission. Buchanan believed that the British would be willing to accept joint military occupation, as proposed by Hornby to Pickett back in August. Scott was to do his best to implement Hornby's plan by reducing the American force to Pickett's company and allow the landing of an equal number of Royal Marines.

Winfield Scott, the audacious young officer who fought the British army on the Niagara peninsula in the War of 1812 and became a United States brigadier general in his twenties, was in his seventies when ordered to the Pacific Northwest on this peace mission. Since his triumph in the Mexican War, Scott had lived a life of comparative leisure at his headquarters in New York. He liked parties, going to the theater, and eating in the best restaurants. He usually arrived at work each morning in full dress uniform, ate an enormous lunch, and spent the afternoon snoozing. His diet and advancing age resulted in a debilitating case of gout. For exercise he relied on horseback riding, but his weight did not allow him to have a solid seat. Just before his trip to the Washington Territory, he was thrown from his horse. He could barely move when he boarded a steamer bound for Panama.

After a smooth voyage and isthmus crossing, Scott left San Francisco October 17 on the *Northerner*, crossed the Columbia River bar and reached Fort Vancouver on October 20. Rather than coming ashore, Scott summoned Harney to his cabin and informed him that he was no longer in charge of the Department of Oregon. Scott was assuming command himself. After talking to Harney and reviewing his correspondence, Scott dismissed Harney's assessment of the San Juan situation and tried to move him out of the area to a position with the army in St. Louis. When the *Northerner* reached Olympia, Scott again refused to disembark to meet Washington Territorial Governor Charles Gholson. At Port Townsend, Scott transferred his headquarters to the USS *Massachusetts*, which had been his flagship during the Mexican War. On the *Massachusetts*, the general had fine, roomy quarters and a glorious cuisine, supplemented by deer, duck, goose and seal, shot by his personal physician and the ship's master.

At Victoria, the British welcomed Scott and treated his envoys with considerably more courtesy than they had extended to Casey and Pickett the month before. Although Douglas initially proposed joint military occupation of San Juan Island, he now preferred civil authority. However, Scott insisted that attempts at civil authority had caused the initial problems of tax collection and customs duties. The general then presented a formal proposal in which each nation would be permitted one company of light infantry (about 100 men), with each commander serving as magistrate to keep peace between the military and civilians of the respective nations. Douglas replied that he could not accept Scott's proposal of joint military occupation without the consent of the British government. However, he offered to withdraw the naval force if Scott would remove Casey's troops. He then reassured Scott that he would not attempt to assume jurisdiction over the island. On November 5, Scott ordered the withdrawal of all the American reinforcements and artillery from San Juan Island. Two days later, the *Massachusetts* steamed into Griffin Bay and the redoubt fired a thirteen-gun salute in Scott's honor. Scott again chose not to disembark. He had managed to arrange peace without once leaving his ship.

Before he left, Scott replaced Pickett with Captain Lewis Cass Hunt. Douglas and Baynes received the joint occupation order in January 1860, and chose a suitable location for the British marines on a sheltered bay on the island's northwest coast that had water and ample space for maneuvers. The 160 marines landed on Garrison Bay on March 21, under the command of Captain George Bazalgette.

Harney was still in command of the Oregon Department. He refused the offered transfer to St. Louis, feeling that support of the officials of the Territory of Washington and the Democratic party would allow him to stay in control. In direct defiance of Scott's orders, he replaced Lewis Cass Hunt and Company D on San Juan Island with Pickett and Company C. When Pickett landed again on April 30, he sent greetings to Bazalgette. Pickett had witnessed diplomacy in action and made every effort to cooperate with the British. Pickett and Bazalgette became friends and handled jurisdiction over civilians and Indians jointly until June 25, 1861 when Pickett, a Virginian, resigned his commission in the United States Army and left to fight for the Confederate States of America.

No one predicted that the joint military occupation of San Juan Island would last for twelve years, but the American Civil War ensued and little thought was given to the sixteen-by-six-mile island in the far off northwest. Relations between the United States and

Great Britain were strained during the Civil War because the British, although not recognizing the Confederacy, had given the rebels indirect support. The particular issue for which the United States asked compensation was damage to United States merchant shipping and whaling caused by the *Alabama* and *Shennandoah*, British-built pirate ships. In order to settle these claims and other unresolved issues between United States and Great Britain, the Treaty of Washington was signed on May 8, 1871. The British negotiators for this treaty included Canadian Prime Minister Sir John A. Macdonald. Macdonald's presence established that the newly-formed Dominion of Canada would at least be a party to settling matters that affected it directly, especially when dealing with the United States. Canada had hoped to receive compensation from the United States for damage caused by Fenian raids in Canada, but Macdonald agreed to cancel these claims in return for having the British guarantee Canadian loans for construction of the Canadian Pacific Railway

Resolution of the water boundary in the San Juan Islands was included in the Treaty of Washington, which turned the matter over to arbitration. Kaiser Wilhelm, Emperor of the newly-established empire of Germany was named arbiter. He appointed a three-man commission, consisting of Professor Heinrich Kiepert, a geographer at the University of Berlin, Councillor Levin Goldschmidt of the Imperial High Court of Commerce, and Dr. Ferdinand Grimm, vice president of the High Court. Dr. Goldschmidt suggested amending the treaty to include the Middle Channel, which he considered to be the logical boundary. Only Haro Strait and Rosario Strait were named in the treaty and United States Secretary of State Hamilton Fish refused to agree to any alteration in the treaty. Haro Strait was chosen in a two-to-one decision and all the San Juan Islands were awarded to the United States, with Dr. Goldschmidt writing a lengthy dissenting opinion.

On November 22, 1872, the Royal Marines packed up their gear and left the 27 structures and formal gardens of English Camp to the Americans. Sir James Douglas, who always considered the San Juan Islands to be British, was no longer in power when the islands were turned over to the United States. His term as governor ended in 1864 and the Hudson's Bay Company was no longer the primary British power in the Pacific Northwest.

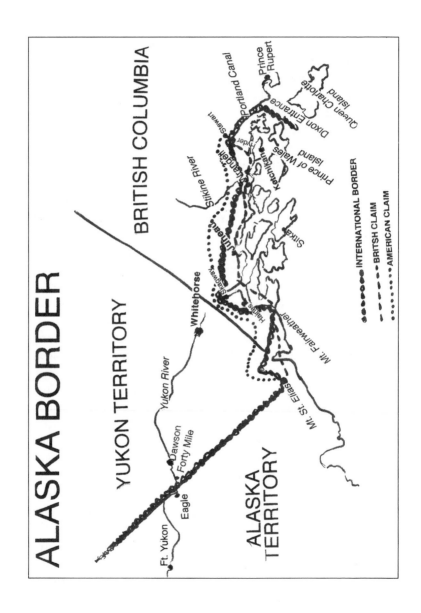

# Alaska Border

Events of March 1867 profoundly influenced the evolution of the northwestern boundary between the United States and Canada. On March 29, Parliament passed the British North American Act, approving the Confederation of the British colonies of Nova Scotia, New Brunswick, Prince Edward Island, and Upper and Lower Canada into the Dominion of Canada. The following day, United States Secretary of State William Henry Seward culminated the purchase of Alaska from Russia. Although these two events were not directly linked, Russia's willingness to sell Alaska to the United States may have been partially motivated by a desire to prevent a takeover of Russian America by Great Britain. The consolidation of the British North American colonies may, on the other hand, have been a means of showing solidarity against any threat of takeover of any of the British colonies by the United States.

British Columbia was not a party to the Confederation in 1867. The purchase of Alaska by the United States presented British Columbia with several options: it could join the Dominion of Canada; petition to join the United States; or remain an independent crown colony. During the Fraser River and Cariboo Gold Rushes in the 1850s, many American prospectors entered British Columbia, but Governor James Douglas managed to keep British control through strict mining laws and the protection of police and courts until his retirement in 1864. Douglas' retirement marked the end of the Hudson's Bay Company's dominance in northwestern North America. Following Confederation, Canada started exercising its own form of manifest destiny, orchestrated by Premier John A. Macdonald and aided when the Hudson's Bay Company turned over Rupert's Land from Upper Canada to British Columbia to the new Dominion of Canada. Macdonald succeeded in wooing British Columbia to join the Dominion in 1871 with the promise of a transcontinental railroad linking the provinces.

The United States bought Alaska under the provision that the boundaries of their new territory would be the same as those stipulated in the 1825 Treaty between Great Britain and Russia. At the time of the 1825 Treaty, the interested parties were the Russian American Company and the Hudson's Bay Company. The Russian American Company was involved in hunting sea otters in the waters around its island settlements while the Hudson's Bay Company was primarily interested in protecting its far-flung inland fur-trading posts extending into the Mackenzie River drainage, which it acquired through merger with the North West Company. Two articles of the 1825 Treaty described the new boundary:

> III. ... Commencing from the southernmost point of the island called Prince of Wales Island, which point lies in the parallel of 54 degrees 40 minutes, north latitude, and between the 131st and 133rd degree of west longitude, the said line shall ascend to the north along the channel called Portland Channel, as far as the point of the continent where it strikes the 56th degree of north latitude; and from this last mentioned point, the line of demarcation shall follow the summit of the mountains situated parallel to the coast as far as the point of intersection of the 141st degree of west longitude; and, finally, from the said point of intersection, the said meridian line of the 141st degree, in its prolongation as far as the Frozen Ocean, shall form the limit between the Russian and British possession on the continent of America to the north-west.

> IV. With reference to the line of demarcation laid down in the preceding Article it is understood:

> 1st. That the island called Prince of Wales Island shall belong wholly to Russia.

> 2nd. That whenever the summit of the mountains which extend in a direction parallel to the coast, from the 56th degree of north latitude to the point of intersection of the 141st degree of west longitude, shall prove to be at the distance of more than 10 marine leagues from the ocean, the limit between the British possessions

and the line of the coast which is to belong to Russia, as above mentioned, shall be formed by a line parallel to the windings of the coast, and which shall never exceed the distance of 10 marine leagues therefrom (about 34.5 miles or 55.6 kilometers).

At the time the treaty was signed, neither country had trading posts close to the new boundary. The Russian settlements were on islands while the Hudson's Bay posts were far inland. Hudson's Bay Governor George Simpson was anxious to expand his territory and to utilize trading boats rather than rely on the inland posts. In mid-June 1837, Peter Skene Ogden arrived at Wrangell aboard the Hudson's Bay brig *Dryad*, intent on establishing a post on the Stikine River farther inland than the 10-league limit. In spite of a provision in the treaty allowing for use of the rivers by both countries, a Russian gunboat blocked the entry to the Stikine River. An appeal to Sitka was answered by a letter in French refusing permission to proceed and suggesting that Hudson's Bay Company representatives visit Sitka after Governor Baron Ferdinand Petrovich von Wrangell returned at the end of August. Negotiations between London and St. Petersburg followed and the incident was finally resolved when the Hudson's Bay Company abandoned their claim for damages as one of the conditions of a lease that would give them control of the mainland portion of the Panhandle lying south and east of a line from Mount Fairweather to Cape Spencer. A ten-year lease was signed on February 6, 1839 by Governor Simpson and Baron Wrangell to start on June 1, 1840. Under terms of the lease, the Russians would give up their trade along the mainland coast in return for an annual rent of two thousand land otter skins taken on the west side of the Rocky Mountains. In addition the Hudson's Bay Company would supply the Russian American Company with agricultural products including flour, pease, barley, salt beef, butter and pork hams at fixed prices and quantities. Prior to the lease, the Russian American Company obtained food and agricultural products from American traders, who were no longer necessary and thereafter excluded from the trade. The lease was later extended for nine years and then for shorter periods until the United States purchased Alaska. The friendly relationship between the Hudson's Bay Company and the Russian American Company continued even during the Crimean War when Russia and Great Britain were at war.

With the lease in place, Hudson's Bay Company activity spread along the Pacific coast. It took over the Russian fort at Wrangell, renaming it Fort Stikine, and established Fort Durham about 10 miles up Taku Inlet. The Company trespassed on Russian territory in the north by establishing Fort Yukon in 1847 at the junction of the Yukon and Porcupine rivers, about 120 miles west of the 141st meridian, and enjoyed a monopoly on the fur-trade throughout what is now British Columbia and the Yukon.

American traders encountered British traders in the spring of 1868 and contested their right to trade in American territory. Early in April 1869, Captain C.W. Raymond of the United States Army Corps of Engineers was ordered to determine the longitude of Fort Yukon. He arrived on July 31 after traveling an estimated 1040 miles from St. Michael. On August 7, the weather cleared sufficiently for Raymond to verify that the post was considerably west of the 141st parallel, and he informed the Hudson's Bay trader that he must vacate the buildings as soon as possible. Raymond, serving as representative of the United States Treasury Department, took over the fort and raised the stars and stripes. The Hudson's Bay Company retreated up the Porcupine River and built a new post to block American traders from invading the Mackenzie River drainage.

Americans entered the area around Fort Yukon to prospect for gold as well as to buy furs, and Leroy McQuesten, Arthur Harper, and Albert Mayo took over as traders at Fort Yukon. The Canada government, aware of the mining activity, established the Yukon expedition in 1887-8 in order to further define the international boundary. William Ogilvie, a government surveyor, undertook the job of marking the 141st parallel on the Yukon River. He completed his first set of observations in late September 1887, and, by the time he abandoned the area in February, he had completed his preliminary calculations of longitude.

Early in February, Ogilvie and two of his men set out to mark the boundary on the Fortymile River, which was the center of placer mining activity in the area. Ogilvie's blazes gave the miners the first warning that their freedom from government control was coming to an end. At the time most of the placer workings were on the Alaska side of the boundary, although the miners were wintering near the border. Ogilvie spent several days explaining to the miners, most of whom were Americans, the strict Canada placer laws. The American miners were accustomed to setting their own laws at miner's meetings.

In the summer of 1895, Ogilvie returned to mark the Alaska Boundary from the Yukon River south to Sixtymile River, a distance of about fifty-six miles. The town at Fortymile had grown and rival trading posts for the Alaska Commercial Company and the North American Transportation and Trading Company faced each other across the Fortymile River. Inspector Charles Constantine of the North-West Mounted Police had arrived with a nineteen-man detachment and was building a post. In addition to his police duties, Constantine had been appointed Canada's government agent, acting as magistrate, gold commissioner, land agent, and collector of customs.

Early in the summer of 1896, Ogilvie received word from Ottawa that negotiations were underway with the United States for a Joint commission to mark the International Boundary and that he was to be Canada's commissioner. However, in September he received word that negotiations for the Joint Commission to survey the 141st meridian had collapsed. For the moment, there was no more work for him to do. He had marked the border in the area where mining was taking place. There was no doubt that the new Klondike gold strikes were in Canada.

While the lease between the Hudson's Bay Company and the Russian American Company was in place between 1840 and 1867, the location of the boundary in southeast Alaska meant very little. In 1872, the government of British Columbia asked the government of Canada to discuss a joint survey of the boundary line with the United States government. Although President Grant mentioned it in his message to Congress, nothing was done because a boundary survey was considered to be too expensive. Secretary of State Hamilton Fish followed the strategy that Secretary of State Calhoun had employed during the period of joint United State and British occupancy prior to the Oregon Treaty and delayed dealing with the boundary question while Americans were establishing a beachhead in the area. In 1873, the placer creeks of the Cassiar gold field were discovered and the Stikine River was the only practical route to the new diggings. By 1874, about fifteen hundred prospectors had joined the rush, and Canada and United States customs agents were squabbling over the collection of duties. There were more discussions about a joint survey, but nothing was done.

The boundary question was raised again in September 1876 when Peter Martin, a prospector who claimed to be a United States citizen was arrested in the Cassiar gold fields for assaulting a police officer. There were no jail facilities in the gold field so two constables were escorting him to Victoria via the Stikine River. At a lunch stop, Martin, who was restrained by handcuffs, managed to grab Constable Frank Beegan's shotgun. A gunfight ensued with both Martin and Beegan missing their targets, but during the struggle a revolver went off grazing Beegan's check. The constables succeeded in subduing Martin and getting him on an outbound British steamer at Wrangell while Beegan received medical attention. Martin insisted that the incident had taken place in Alaska and that he was held illegally by Canada's constables.

Six weeks after the incident, Secretary of State Hamilton Fish protested to the British ambassador in Washington, setting off a lengthy chain of communication from Washington to London and then to the governor-general in Ottawa and finally to Canada's government. At Martin's trial in December, even though it was evident that no one actually knew in which country the incident had taken place, the jury found Martin guilty of assaulting an officer and the judge sentenced him to an additional twenty-one months of hard labor.

Finally, in March 1877, the surveyor-general of Canada, instructed Joseph Hunter, a civil engineer from Victoria, to mark his impression of the boundary. Hunter placed two monuments along the Stikine River, one approximately 54 miles upstream, which he considered to be ten leagues distant from the general line of the coast, and another 24.74 miles upstream, which he estimated to be on the line following the summit of mountains running parallel to the coast. As far as Hunter and the constables present during the Martin incident could ascertain, the incident had taken place about eight and a half miles within American territory. After more diplomatic correspondence, Canada's minister of justice recommended that Martin be released because he had been conveyed through United States territory without authorization. Soon after Martin was set free, he was jailed in Washington State jail for attempting to smuggle a case of brandy from Canada.

In April 1884, William H. Dall of the United States Coast and Geodetic Survey raised the boundary question in a prophetic letter to George M. Dawson of the Geological Survey of Canada: "The matter of the boundary should be stirred up. The language of the treaty of 1825 is so indefinite that were the region included for any cause to become suddenly of evident value, or if any serious international question were to arise regarding jurisdiction, there would be no means of settling it by the treaty. There being no natural boundary and the continuous range of mountains parallel to the coast shown on Vancouver's charts like a long caterpillar having no existence as such, the United States would undoubtedly fall back on the 'line parallel to the windings of the coast and which shall never exceed the distance of ten marine leagues therefrom' of the treaty. ... Before the question has attained any importance, it should be referred to a committee of geographers, a survey should be made and a new treaty should be made stating determinable boundaries."

Although both Canadians and Americans realized that something had to be done about marking the border, nothing happened until the Convention of July 22, 1892 when the United States and Canada agreed to begin planning field work to mark the border. The United States commissioner chosen was T.C. Mendenhall, superintendent of the U.S. Coast and Geodetic Survey and W.F. King, chief astronomer of Canada's Department of the Interior, was the designated representative for Canada. Each country provided its own field party and covered expenses. Initially a representative of the other country was to accompany each party, but this practice was discontinued after the first season. The American parties were assigned to mark boundaries along the major rivers, while the Canadians surveyed the intervening areas. Each country had its own interests in mind. The United States parties planned to erect markers ten leagues from the coast, while the Canadians were intent on proving that summits parallel to the coast did exist and that they were very close to tidewater.

The Canada parties used photo-topographic methods to establish camera stations located high enough in the coastal mountains to afford a clear view of the mountains and valleys farther inland. Much of the initial work on this new technique had been done by Canada's surveyor general, E. Deville. The new method replaced plane-table methods and the photographs obtained contained information that could be used later to revise or complete the mapping. At the end of the 1895 season, both countries produced maps of the mainland portion of the panhandle. The Canada maps were topographic maps with contour lines, while the American maps simply indicated some of the larger peaks. The maps reflected each country's interpretation of the 1825 Treaty, the Canada ones suggesting a range of mountains, while the American ones showed a random distribution of mountains. The surveyors had done their job, but the maps were filed away for future reference.

Soon the disputed territory acquired additional importance. George Carmack discovered gold in the Klondike streams in 1896, and the area at the head of Lynn Canal became valuable as the access to the interior gold fields. In August 1896, the United States declared Dyea a sub port of entry and soon expanded the designation to Skagway. In the meanwhile, Canada planned to establish custom stations at the Chilkoot and White passes. Both countries claimed the boom towns of Skagway and Dyea at the head of Lynn Canal. Each country collected custom duties from stampeders who had purchased equipment in the other country.

In late February 1898, Royal Canada Mounted Police detachments raised the Union Jack at newly constructed posts in both Chilkoot and White passes and began collecting duty. The Mounted Police were in full control of the two main routes to the Klondike and demanded that each man entering the territory have a year's supply of food. At about the same time, four companies of United States troops were posted at Skagway and Dyea. In May 1898, the North-West Mounted Police established a post on the Dalton Trail that ran from Chilkat Inlet over the Chilkat Pass, reaching the Yukon River near Carmacks.

As the pressure of mining in the area increased, in October 1899, United States Secretary of State John Hay and Sir Reginald Tower, British charge in Washington, decided to fix provisional boundaries pending more definitive negotiations. The decision to make the Chilkoot and White Passes provisional boundaries was made quickly, but an American demand to run the Chilkat provisional border along the south bank of the Klehini River meant that the Porcupine gold camp would be in American territory.

The intensity of the Klondike gold rush diminished over the next two years and many prospectors left the area. No further definitive negotiations took place while Great Britain and Canada were involved fighting the Boer War in South Africa. The Canadians hoped for the boundary decision to be referred to a neutral arbitrator, but the Americans would not agree to arbitration. Americans also reject-ed a proposal to allow the Canadians a corridor to the coast with a port at Pyramid Harbor on Chilkat Inlet. President Theodore Roos-evelt was convinced that there was no credibility in the Canada claim and threatened to take the territory by force unless some mutual agreement could be reached.

In a final attempt to achieve an agreement, Secretary of State John Hay and Sir Michael Herbert, the British ambassador, signed the Hay-Herbert Treaty on January 24, 1903. The treaty called for a tri-bunal consisting of "six impartial jurists of repute, who shall consider judicially the questions submitted to them, each of whom shall first subscribe an oath that he will impartially consider the arguments and evidence presented to the Tribunal, and will decide thereupon according to his true judgment. Three members of the Tribunal shall be appointed by His Britannic Majesty and three by the president of the United States. All questions considered by the Tribunal, includ-ing the final award, shall be decided by a majority of the members thereof." The Tribunal members were to answer seven questions deal-ing with the Anglo-Russian Treaty of 1825.

1. What is the point of commencement of the border line?
2. What channel is the Portland Channel?
3. What course should the line take from the point of commence-ment to the entrance to Portland Channel?
4. To what point on the 56th parallel is the line to be drawn from the head of Portland Channel, and what course should it follow?
5. Was it the intention and meaning of the Convention of 1825 that there should remain in the exclusive possession of Russia, a continuous strip of coast on the mainland not exceeding 10 ma-rine leagues from the coast.
6. If the question above is answered in the negative, was it the intention that the strip of land be measured from the line of direc-tion of the mainland coast or from the heads of inlets?
7. What, if they exist, are the mountains referred to as situated parallel to the coast?

President Roosevelt chose Senator Henry Cabot Lodge, former Senator George Turner of Washington, and Secretary of War Elihu

Root as the American representatives. The Canadians objected strongly because these men did not appear to be impartial jurists of repute and Lodge was an outspoken opponent of the Canada claim. British selections were two Canadians, Sir Louis Jette, former member of the Quebec Supreme Court, and Allen B. Aylesworth, a Toronto lawyer, and Lord Alverstone, Britain's Lord Chief Justice. These appointments would appear to have more judicial backgrounds, but the Canadians were probably as partisan as the Americans. Lord Alverstone had the swing vote and he was urged by the British government to give primary concern to British relations with the United States. The actual territory involved was on the other side of the world and of little importance to Great Britain.

The Tribunal was actually little more than a cover for Roosevelt's pressure tactics. In a letter to Supreme Court Justice Oliver Wendell Holmes he stated his position that, although there were several points to discuss about the position of the actual boundary , "the claim of the Canadians for access to deep water along any part of the Canada coast is just exactly as indefensible as if they should now suddenly claim the island of Nantucket." He made it clear that, if the Tribunal failed to reach a decision, he would ask Congress to authorize him to "run the line as we claim it by our own people, without further regard to the attitude of England and Canada." He further indicated that "there will be no arbitration of the matter." Justice Holmes and Senator Lodge spread Roosevelt's threat throughout the British government.

Members of the Tribunal and their staffs congregated in London in late August 1903 and oral arguments began on September 15. As the Americans and Canadians presented their cases, it was evident that much of the controversy centered around the definition of "coast" and "ocean." The Canadians contended that the 1825 Treaty meant the word "coast" to refer to the general direction of the coast, not including the inlets. They referred to the waters of inlets less than six miles (twice the three-mile limit) in width as territorial waters rather than as "ocean." The Americans, on the other hand contended that the word "coast" included shores of all inlets and that the waters of these inlets were "ocean." The Canadians, therefore, reasoned that the strip of mainland American territory, referred to by the French term "lisiere," would cut across the inlets and not be continuous. The Americans contended that the "lisiere" awarded to the Russians in the 1825 Treaty was meant to be continuous. One of the arguments the Americans used to support their claim was that the early maps drawn by the Russians showed a continuous "lisiere" around the inlets and that the British never complained that these maps were not accurate. Lacking maps more accurate than Vancouver's map, which had sketched a mountain chain following the coast, some subsequent maps perpetuated a continuous mainland "lisiere." Prior to the emergence of British Columbia and Canada as political entities with territorial imperatives, it is easy to understand why the British took little note of the representation of a continuous "lisiere" on maps. The Hudson's Bay Company was Great Britain's agent in the area and Governor Simpson had solved any problems of access to the ocean by the mutually advantageous contract with the Russian American Company that gave British interests control of the mainland coast.

Inaccuracy of the early maps and a lack of geographical knowledge was responsible for another point of contention. The negotiators of the 1825 Treaty apparently assumed that Portland Channel reached the 56th parallel north latitude, and so the Tribunal had to decide on the route the boundary would take between the head of Portland Channel and the 56th parallel. The Americans contended that it should follow the direction of Portland Channel to the northeast, while the Canadians thought it should go in a northwesterly direction until it intersected a mountain chain on the 56th parallel. There was mutual agreement that Portland Channel, as designated by Vancouver, was the narrow deep-water passage that ran north of Wales and Pearse Islands, but there were two additional small islands, Sitklan and Kanagunut, at the entrance to Portland Channel. Initially the Americans had tried to claim all four islands, and Americans had built stone storehouses on both Wales and Pearse islands and a cannery on Wales Island. The Canadians also claimed the four islands.

The three Americans combined to present their judgments, which agreed completely with the American case. The two Canadians wrote separate conclusions and generally agreed with the Canadian presentations. Everything rested on the judgment of Lord Alverstone. He agreed with the American case that the "lisiere" was meant to be continuous and that the border above Portland Channel should pass in a northeasterly direction to the 56th parallel. However, he disagreed with the Americans about disregarding reference to a chain of mountains and designated certain mountain peaks on the maps that should be considered as part of a mountain chain running parallel to the coast. The border would then follow a line connecting these peaks and would result in a compromise between the Canada and American lines.

A final decision concerned the four islands at the entrance to Portland Channel. Although Alverstone had appeared to agree that all four islands should be Canada's, his final decision agreed with the American claim that the boundary line should pass between Wales and Siklan Islands. The Tribunal gave Wales and Pearse Islands to the Canadians but Sitklan and Kanagunut Islands to the Americans. This decision was the final blow to the Canadians and Jette and Aylesworth refused to sign the Tribunal report. Although the Canadians claimed that American ownership of the small islands would strategically block Canada's entrance to Portland Canal, the real blow was to their pride. Ownership of these islands was Canada's last chance to save face. Years later in his memoirs, Turner explained that a careful reading of Vancouver's journals convinced him that Vancouver had entered the area between Wales and Sitkan islands. Roosevelt referred to the islands as "Turner's twins" and praised him saving valuable territory for his country.

Newspapers throughout Canada rallied to the support of Jette and Aylesworth in their refusal to sign the Tribunal report. The Canadian sentiment is best summarized in Francis H. Turnock's article in the November 7, 1903 issue of *Outlook* entitled "The Consequences of the Alaskan Boundary Award From a Canadian Point of View."

The callousness, the selfishness, and the bad faith with which Canadians consider Britain has treated Canada in this matter will long rankle in the breasts of Canadians. It is bound to affect Canada's destiny. What the ultimate outcome may be, it is perhaps too early yet to predict. But it will sensibly loosen the tie which binds Canada to Great Britain. It will quench the spirit of Imperialism which has for some time been growing in Canada in spite of much discouragement from Great Britain. Canadians now realize how little their services in the cause of the Empire have been appreciated. … Great Britain may think she has scored a diplomatic triumph in conciliating the United States. She may yet find that the alienation of her chief colony was a tremendous price to pay for that diplomatic triumph. … We may as well go in for annexation, body and breeches, if Great Britain is going to allow us to be annexed piecemeal. Independence will be the idea to which Canadians will naturally turn. The outcome much depends on the future attitude of the United States. There is re-annexation sentiment in Canada today as there was, to some extent, a dozen years ago. The United States killed what sentiment of that sort there was by attempting, as Canadians believed, to coerce and bully Canada. It is possible that, in considering what course would be best for Canada to take were once British connection dissolved, a party in favour of annexation might again arise in Canada. Were that so, the choice between independence and annexation would be decided very much by events, in connection with which the attitude of the United States would be a most important factor. It is at present, as has been said, impossible to forecast the outcome. What is at present certain is that there will be strong reaction against Imperialism and very pronounced manifestation of the fact that the tie binding Canada to Britain has been dangerously strained.

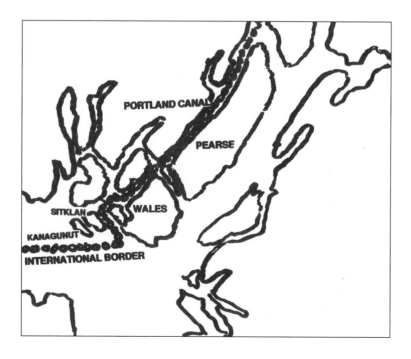

# The Border Today

More than a hundred years have passed since the resolution of major disputes along the United States/Canada border. On the border today, Americans and Canadians usually work well together and are often interdependent. The border was often ignored until recent emphasis on security has created problems.

## NORTHEAST BORDER

The Aroostook Valley Country Club, located a few miles from Fort Fairfield, Maine, and near Four Falls, New Brunswick, was laid out with the golf course and clubhouse in Canada during the 1920s when the United States was in the throes of prohibition. The parking lot, however, was placed in the United States. The Stars and Stripes and the Maple Leaf still fly together over the clubhouse, but Canadian golfers have to detour for miles to a border control station in order to park their cars at the course.

A similar problem has arisen at Derby Line, Vermont, and Stanstead, Quebec, where the Haskell Library and Opera House was built on the border in 1904 as a symbol of Canadian-American friendship. The original owners were a binational couple. Charles Haskell from Derby Line owned several lumber mills. Mrs. Haskell was born in Canada. The building was offered to the communities by Martha Haskell and her son as a memorial to Charles Haskell. The upper half of the building is a scale model of the old Boston opera house. About a third of the 450 seats and the stage are in Canada. The black line denoting the international border is carefully marked in the polished wooden floor. The Haskells' intent was that people on both sides of the border would have use of the facility, which is now a designated historic site. Library patrons from either side of the border always have used the facility without going through border security. The entrance to the facility is in the United States, all the books are on the Canada side and half of them are in French. The library isn't the only evidence of the interdependence of these two communities because they also share water and sewer systems as well as emergency services. Recently, the United States Border Patrol has proposed to erect barricades to close streets which have historically crossed the border between Derby Line and Stanstead. Town meetings have discussed the situation, and the protests have been well covered on Vermont Public Television. Committees from the two towns are studying the problem, but doubt that barricading the three streets with flower pots will have any impact on security.

These are not isolated situations. Private homes and farms straddle the border in many locations. Marion and Nickalaj Pedersen have lived on their Perth-Andover, New Brunswick, potato farm for 53 years. Their driveway is in Canada, but the road to it is in the United States. Brown Road is a local curiosity because it twists back and forth across the border. The Pedersens are the only Canadians living along the road. An American customs agent threatened to arrest Mrs. Pedersen for illegal border crossing in 2003. She escaped prosecution, and eventually got special dispensation for herself and her husband to cross the street without getting into trouble. No such permission was granted for anyone coming to visit or make a delivery. They have to report at the official border crossing miles away.

New Brunswick was particularly concerned when the American government increased security at its international borders prior to the invasion of Iraq in 2003. The province's economy depends on trade with Americans. Eighty-five percent of the province's exports are reported to cross the Maine- New Brunswick border.

These are examples of places where the existing international border was either accidently or purposefully ignored. A different situation exists in northern Maine where the international border, adjudicated in the Webster-Ashburton Treaty of 1842, splits an existing community in the upper St. John River valley between Maine and New Brunswick. At the time of the treaty, this community, which called itself the Republic of Madawaska, consisted of Acadians, who had originally settled along the Bay of Fundy, and some American settlers. Subsequently, more Acadians and Quebecois have moved into the area along with Americans, English, Scots, and Irish. As soon as the Webster-Ashburton Treaty divided the Republic of Madawaska between Maine and New Brunswick, Quebec and New Brunswick began bickering over ownership of the land on the north side of the upper St. John River. The bickering between the two British colonies persisted for fifteen years until it was settled by dividing the area again, with Quebec receiving the northern half. The narrow southern half is now the New Brunswick panhandle.

Descendents of original settlers still live in the New Brunswick panhandle. Jean Baker White grew up in Fort Kent. Her father, a descendent of American John Baker, was superintendent of schools for Frenchville and St. Agatha, both in the St. John valley, in the 1960s. Superintendent Baker understood French, but refused to speak it unless absolutely necessary, while his French Canadian wife "floated between the two languages." Jean and her four siblings understood French but rarely spoke it. After attending high school and college in England, Jean returned to the area and married Jerry White, a direct descendent of Rene LeBlanc, who was the king's notary public in Grand Pre before the Grande Derangement. During a census in the early 1900s, those LeBlancs living on the United States side of the border were summarily renamed White. The Rossignols became Nightingales and many Levesques were turned into Bishops. Others altered the spelling of their names to appear less French. From 1990 to 2001, Jerry White held the position of superintendent of schools for the St. John valley towns of Frenchville and St. Agatha, where the home language was 90% French. The people "either felt absolute shame or total pride in their French background," so the Whites sought to make French an asset rather than a liability.

People living in the New Brunswick panhandle still refer to the area as the Republic of Madawaska. Madawaska is the Maliseet Indian word for porcupine. A giant porcupine, "Typique," the mascot of La Republique de Madawaska, leads the grand march during the annual Foire Brayonne, a five-day Acadian celebration in Edmundston. The mayor of Edmundston, which is reported to be the largest French-speaking city outside of Quebec, is the honorary president of La Republique de Madawaska. Canadian humorist Will Ferguson reports counting six flags from his hotel room window in Edmundston during the celebration: the Canada maple leaf, the fleur-de-lis, the stars and stripes, the New Brunswick boat carrying

Loyalists, the State of Maine's pine tree, and finally, a modern version of John Baker's pouncing eagle, the flag he hoisted over the Republic of Madawaska on the 4th of July in 1827. When asked about the symbolism of the Madawaska Flag, the mayor of Edmundston explained, "The eagle is for this powerful neighbor of ours, the United States, the white background is for the openness of the Madawaska landscape and its people, a purified crossbreed of Acadians, French-Canadians, aboriginals and Anglo-Saxons. The six stars represent the six founding peoples, the Natives, the Acadians, the Quebeckers, the English, the Scots, and the Irish."

Not as many people live in the southern part of the disputed territory, allocated to Maine by the Webster-Ashburton Treaty. Historically, there were farms on the St. John and Allagash rivers, but they have since reverted to forest. Most of the land is owned by large American lumber companies. The forest land is traversed by private roads, some of which cross the border and are granted special permission to enter Canada. The manager of one of these lumber companies commented, "I have always found it striking that, after driving for hours through nothing but Maine timberland with almost no houses, no electric or telephone lines or any other utility type services, you reach the Quebec border, peak the hill and head down to the U.S.-Canada border at St. Pamphile looking at mostly open farmland, lots of churches and numerous small communities." In Maine, private landowners have actively managed these lands for over 160 years with no difficulty from the Canada side. They use a mix of American and Canadian workers to harvest and truck trees to mills, which are mostly in Canada because of the reduced trucking distance. The lumber companies relied on French Canadian workers during World War II because Quebec did not draft them. Originally logs were transported to mills on the St. John River, but laws have subsequently changed, so transport of logs on the river is prohibited.

Entrepreneurs, like David Pingree, began acquiring forest land in northern Maine in the early 1800s when six-mile-square surveyed townships were sold by the District of Maine, prior to statehood in 1820. Later the State of Maine conducted land sales to raise money, but hoped to promote settlement by allocating acres for public purposes. This design was copied later by the federal government in disposing of lands in the west.

Along the border west of the Republic of Madawaska and the Maine timber lands lies the Northeast Kingdom, comprised of the three northeastern Vermont counties, Essex, Orleans, and Caledonia. The Northeast Kingdom does not have a king, but it does have a regional author, Howard Frank Mosher, who has introduced readers in Canada and the United States to the countryside and rural traditions of the area around Lake Memphremagog, which is bisected by the international border. Some of Mosher's ten novels, notably *A Stranger in the Kingdom*, deal with serious subjects such as racial intolerance. Mosher's most recent novel, *On Kingdom Mountain*, depicts the area in a more humorous manner, presenting memorable characters like Miss Jane Hubbell Kinneson, who regularly consults life-sized carvings of her ancestors while fighting the encroachment of a new international super highway. The border area in Quebec, know as the Eastern Townships, is not officially part of the Northeast Kingdom, but French Canadians are essential characters in Mosher's novels and regional activities, like whisky smuggling, are prominent elements in his plots. In *Disappearances* Mosher introduces one of these Canadians: "Somewhere in his travels, he acquired the name Quebec Bill, pronounced with the hard French 'k.' He ran an impromptu delivery service, carrying notes, invitations, packages, covered dishes, and word-of-mouth messages. Sometimes he crossed the border several times a day. He was never more than twenty-five or thirty miles north or south of the forty-fifth parallel, that arbitrary demarcation that had stretched through five generations of our family like a five-thousand-mile umbilical cord to the past, along which he had sojourned all his life and which existed only on paper but represented all the geographical and historical continuity he had ever known." The towns of Newport and St. Johnsbury are in the Northeast Kingdom as are Derby Line, Vermont, and Stanstead, Quebec, which share the Haskell library and opera house.

After the American naval victory on Lake Champlain during the War of 1812, the Americans started to build a fort at Rouses Point on the northwestern shore of the lake. Construction of the fort was stopped temporarily when the forty-fifth parallel was resurveyed and the fort was found to be above the actual parallel and, therefore, in Canada. Construction was completed after the Webster-Ashburton Treaty stipulated that the original survey line should be used as the

International Boundary rather than the true forty-fifth parallel. Local people called it "Fort Blunder," but it was officially named Fort Montgomery. The fort was intended to hold 800 men, but was only occupied by a small company during the American Civil War. The granite was removed to build the causeway across the lake and the guns were removed in 1910. It had a brief career as a tourist attraction, but since has deteriorated. Canadian author, Marian Bosford Fraser, visited the old fort while writing *Walking the Line, Travels Along the Canadian American Border.* In her book, she describes the remains: "I walked past a series of archways with straight granite sides, their tops shaped with red brick, some still with wooden ceilings. At right angles to the row of arches there is the main body of the fort, a two-story structure, with galleries and walkways connecting open rooms, still dry and warm, home to pigeons who flew up startled at my appearance. Big round portholes open to the south. The site is a marvelous combination of childhood fantasy fort or something grander and more mysterious. … There is extensive defacement and deterioration, and not a single interpretive sign, but the fort retains splendour this autumn morning. I recall a visit to a goblin's castle in the border region of Scotland, a ruin ignored, a monument unsaluted, a place in which imagination can re-create a history."

## GREAT LAKES BORDER

The Treaty of Paris envisioned a straight line bisecting Lake Ontario, Lake Erie, Lake Huron, and Lake Superior as the International Boundary, with the boundary then following the middle of the connecting rivers and channels. The United States and Canada abut each other at three points along this section of the border; the Niagara Peninsula, the Detroit/Windsor area, and Sault Ste. Marie. All three of these pressure points figured crucially in the War of 1812. The rest of that war was fought on the lakes themselves. Shipwreck hunters claim to have discovered a ships' graveyard with four War of 1812 wrecks, possibly including Commodore James Yeo's flagship, on the murky lake bottom near Kingston, Ontario, where they were scuttled years after the war. They expect that the discovery will generate international interest during the bicentennial of the War of 1812.

Generals Winfield Scott and John Harvey would not recognize the Niagara Peninsula, where they fought each other for three years during the War of 1812. The falls are still there, but only about half of the water that enters the Niagara River actually passes over the falls. The rest of the water is diverted to hydroelectric plants on both the United States and Canada sides of the river. The power and beauty of Niagara Falls is manipulated by switches in the International Power Authority control tower above the falls on the Canada side. The quantities of water in each of eighteen sluice gates is monitored and adjusted every fifteen minutes. The Falls have a day shift of 100,000 cubic feet per second from 8AM to 10PM in the summer.

The night shift allows half that amount of water to the Falls from 10PM to 8AM in the summer and all the time during the winter. The Welland Canal allows ships to pass from Lake Erie to Lake Ontario, with eight massive locks to handle the 327 feet of difference between the lakes.

The patriotism usually found in historical battlegrounds is muted on the Niagara Peninsula because there are two sides to the story. Fort Erie, Fort George, and Fort Niagara stand as mute witnesses to their dramatic past. On Queenston Heights, the Brock Monument stands to remind Canadians of their first intimations of nationhood. The rest of the Niagara Peninsula, in both the United States and Canada, has become primarily tourist traps. English poet Rupert Brooks visited the area in 1906 and wrote: "The human race, apt as a child to destroy what it admires, has done its best to surround the Falls with every distraction, incongruity, and vulgarity. Hotels, powerhouses, bridges, trams, picture post cards, sham legends, stalls, booths, rifle-galleries, and side-shows frame them about."

Although both Ontario and New York have independently established parks, the situation hasn't changed. Marian Botsford Fraser describes Clifton Hill, the famous Street of Horrors in Niagara Falls, Ontario in her book: In one short block: "Houdini's Hall of Fame, Reg's Candy Kitchen, the House of Frankenstein, a Burger King, Ripley's Believe it or Not, Movieland Wax Museum, Castle Dracula, the Louis Tussard Wax Museum, the Guiness Museum of World Records, Sports Hall of Fame, the tower ride, a miniature golf course, and Circus World. On Clifton Hill you can picture yourself going over the falls in a barrel."

Little remains in the Detroit/Windsor area to remind Americans and Canadians of the battles fought there during the War of 1812. The border goes underground in the yellow-tiled Windsor/Detroit Tunnel. This is appropriate in a way since the border crossing here was an important part of the Underground Railway that transported black slaves to freedom in Canada prior to the American Civil War, Great Britain refused to enact a reciprocal fugitive slave agreement with the United States, and an estimated forty thousand black fugitives settled in communities like Amherstburg, Sandwich, and Windsor. Many returned to the United States after the Emancipation Proclamation but a vital black community remains around Windsor.

Marian Botsford Fraser contrasts the deterioration and crime in downtown Detroit with the old-world British charm of much smaller Windsor, summing it up: "Windsor/Detroit is a clear visual metaphor for Canadian/American relations; our cultures eyeball one another across the Detroit River as we do nowhere else along the border. In this odd pairing of a vibrant, volatile city and a low-profile lunch-bucket town, you see Canada and the United States at work together daily; close, but very distinct, rubbing shoulders industrially and economically, but very different culturally. People of Windsor and along the shores of Lake Erie are clearer than Anglophones elsewhere in Canada about their distinctive identity."

The third point of contact between Canada and the United States along the Great Lakes portion of the border is at Sault Ste. Marie between Lake Huron and Lake Superior. During the War of 1812, the American fort on Mackinac Island was taken over by the British, but returned to the United States in the Treaty of Ghent. The British then established a fort on Drummond Island, but little remains in the area today to identify this battleground. The main activity at Sault Ste. Marie now is at the locks, through which fleets of cargo ships pass daily. Before the locks were built in 1853, the Sault was a provisioning point for native fishermen and fur traders. Now there are four large American locks, the MacArthur, the Poe, the Davis, and the Sabin. The Canadians built a small old-fashioned lock in 1895.

## THE FORTY-NINTH PARALLEL

The impetus to build a Canada lock came from a border incident. In 1870, the government of Upper Canada sent troops to the Red River community where mixed-blood Metis residents under the leadership of Louis Riel had conquered Fort Garry, at present day Winnipeg, Manitoba. The Metis were protesting the transfer of Rupert's Land from the Hudson's Bay Company to the new Dominion of Canada. The Canadian troops arrived at Sault Ste. Marie in two ships, but the second ship was not permitted to pass through the American locks in defiance of a long-standing agreement between the United States and Great Britain. The order to stop the ship came from the United States State Department as a gesture of sympathy for Louis Riel, who was supported by Americans living in Pembina, just south of the 49th parallel. Before the Canadian Pacific Railroad was completed in the 1880s, the main access to the Red River colony was up the Red River from the United States through Pembina and some residents of the area saw the Metis rebellion as an opportunity to promote annexation to the United States.

Enos Stutsman, a lawyer and Dakota territorial legislator from Pembina, gave Riel legal advise and tried to persuade the Metis to seek annexation to the United States. However, the Red River settlers decided to join the new Canada confederation instead, and, in May 1870, Manitoba became a Canada province. Louis Riel fled to the United States, where he lived in exile until 1885, when he led the ill-fated Meti rebellion at Batoche, Saskatchewan.

Three years after the Red River rebellion, American and British surveyors arrived in Pembina to begin the official survey of the 49th parallel. George M. Dawson began his career as a young member of the surveying team. In subsequent years he would be involved in various areas along the border including Alaska, Trained in Montreal and at the Royal School of Mines in London, Ontario, he wrote a journal which described the birds, animals, and plants of this little-known area, and contained technical descriptions of the geological formations along the border.

Dawson went to considerable effort to explain the geology of Turtle Mountain on the border between Manitoba and North Dakota. After analyzing the shorelines of small lakes and pebbles in the streams, he concluded that Turtle Mountain was a collection of debris drawn from areas as far away as the Rocky Mountains, deposited by a grounded iceberg. Turtle Mountain is now the site of the International Peace Garden, which was established in 1932 near the geographical center of North America, straddling the border between the United States and Canada. In 1928, Dr. Henry J. Moore, a Canada-born horticulturist, came up with the idea of creating a garden "where the people of two countries could share the glories found in a lovely garden and the pleasure found in warm friendships." The International Peace Garden is owned by a private, nonprofit organization that equally represents Canada and the United States. Of the 2400 acres set aside for the garden, about 34 acres are intensely landscaped. The area includes two lakes and about 2000 deer.

Marian Botsford Fraser visited the International Peace Garden several years ago and noted: "Right on the boundary, there is the Peace Tower, the Peace Chapel and formal gardens. On the north side, there is the Canadian Natural Drive, on the south side, the United States Cultural Drive. There is only one entrance. The International Peace Garden is completely fortified, surrounded by thick, matted checkerboard wire fencing, joining posts built like chimneys." She contrasts the North Dakota side where there is an artificial lake and low profile buildings, a floral clock by Bulova, and a tablet containing the Ten Commandments, dedicated by Carelton Heston, with the 1451 acres of "minimally contoured wilderness" on the Manitoba side.

A long relatively uncontrolled border can be an invitation to smuggling, particularly when one side has something the other side wants, as was the case with whiskey during Prohibition in the United States. Moose Jaw, Saskatchewan, established in 1882 as a divisional point on the Canadian Pacific Railway, owed much to the illegal whiskey trade during its formative years. As the terminus of the Soo Line, which connected it to Chicago, Moose Jaw's River Street, according to Will Ferguson, "was an all-night carnival of brothels and bootleg joints, of pool rooms and faro games, jazz bands and poker brawls, and girls who waved at you from windows. … There had been whispers of bootlegger hideaways and passageways beneath the streets of Moose Jaw for years; a network of tunnels that ran from the railroads to River Street, and from the warehouses to the hotels and gambling dens." Today a visitor can tour the Tunnels of Moose Jaw, which may not be entirely authentic. The tour company suggests that the original tunnels were built by Chinese families, driven underground by persecution, and then taken over by bootleggers. During Prohibition bootleggers and gangsters did make Moose Jaw their base. The post office was robbed in broad daylight and some members of the police department ended up in prison. There were shootouts, ambushes, and car chases across the prairies. The wild Prohibition days came to an end in the Great Depression of the 1930s. The prairies were already facing a devastating drought when the American stock market collapsed.

Strict adherence to the 49th parallel as the border between the United States and Canada has resulted in several instances where United States territory can only be accessed on the ground by passing through Canada. The state of Alaska, which is more frequently accessed by air or water, will be discussed later. Two other small areas are Angle Township in Minnesota and Point Roberts in Washington state.

The Northwest Angle was created when Lake Itasca, the source of the Mississippi River was found to be south of the farthest northwest corner of the Lake of the Woods and the boundary line was, therefore, established as a straight line from the northwest corner of the Lake of the Woods to the 49th parallel. Angle Township, a part of Lake of the Woods County, Minnesota, is the only part of the United States, except Alaska, that is north of the 49th parallel. According to the United States Census Bureau, Angle Township has a total area of 596 square miles, of which 123 square miles, including several islands, is land. The 2000 census noted 118 people living on the mainland and 34 on the islands. The township has the last one-room school in the state. The school attendance varies seasonally and students above the sixth grade are bused about 130 miles round trip each day to Warroad, Minnesota. In 1998, a move to allow the part of Minnesota accessible only though Canada to secede from the United States was opposed by leaders of Red Lake Indian Reservation, which holds land in the Northwest Angle.

Point Roberts, an unincorporated community in Whatcom County, Washington, is located on the southernmost tip of the Tsawwassen Peninsula, south of Delta, British Columbia. Point Roberts, named by George Vancouver for his friend Henry Roberts, has its own ZIP code, 98281, but can be reached from the rest of the United States only by traveling through Canada or crossing Boundary Bay. The decision to accept the 49th parallel as the international boundary was made without precise knowledge of the geography of the area. When surveying the line, the British government realized that the peninsula of Point Roberts would be an isolated part of the United States. The British Foreign Office suggested that Point Roberts be left to Britain and that equivalent compensation be made by alteration of the boundary line elsewhere. Point Roberts, however, remained part of the United States.

The Point Roberts Peninsula has an area of 4,884 square miles and a population of 1,820 according to the 2000 census. The original settlers were Icelandic farmers and fishermen, who came down from Victoria in search of cheap land. They built farms, worked in fish canneries, and caught salmon in fish traps that decimated the local fish stocks until they were banned in the 1930s. Canadians are still flocking to Point Roberts for summer cottages, cheap gasoline, and excellent wine stores. A handful of bars and nightclubs are popular with visitors from Greater Vancouver, although this popularity diminished slightly when Sunday drinking was legalized in British Columbia. Hundreds of Vancouver businesses and individuals rent postal boxes at the Point Roberts post office because it is a convenient way to receive mail and parcels from the United States without paying cross-border shipping costs. Point Roberts Primary School for kindergarten though second grade is the only school on the peninsula. Older American children take a forty-minute bus ride into British Columbia and then back into the United States at the Blaine, Washington, border crossing. After the September 11, 2001, attacks on the United States, school transportation became a problem because of long delays at the border, however, school buses are regularly given right of way. Canadian children living in Point Roberts attend school in British Columbia.

## THE SAN JUAN ISLANDS

The San Juan Islands have become a tourist destination and popular retirement area for Americans. On the internet, the islands advertise 247 days of sunshine and only half the rain of Seattle, and recommend bicycling, kayaking, beach combing, whale watching, and art galleries. Washington State ferries have regular service to the San Juan Islands from Anacortes , Washington, with a connecting route to Sydney. British Columbia. Tourists are cautioned to bring passports or proof of citizenship with them if planning to go on to Canada.

On pastoral San Juan Island, tourists can relive the quirky history of the island by visiting the two American National Park sites on the grounds of the American and English camps during the years of joint occupancy following the Pig War. The National Park Service acquired both campsites in 1966. The first archaeological excavation at English Camp was undertaken in 1870 under the auspices of the University of Washington. Over the next nine years, University of Idaho students excavated surface sites encompassing nearly the entire living area of the camp, including the four surviving structures: the barracks, commissary, blockhouse, and hospital—as well as the terraces on Officers' Hill and the beach and parade ground east of the barracks. As a National Park Service unit, English Camp is a major attraction to tourists on San Juan Island. Nearly 20,000 people visit the grounds and buildings annually. Each summer, re-enactors from the United States and Canada recreate on the parade grounds the visits that the camps exchanged almost a century and a half ago. On the small hill above English Camp, a little cemetery contains the bodies of seven young Englishmen, commemorated by plain plaques explaining three drownings and one accidental shooting. When Marian Botsford Fraser visited the area, she was struck by the stark contrast between the two camps. "The American Camp is a bleak, wind-swept prairie that looks as if it should have been a battlefield, there is not a single building, just a scattering of modest, woeful plaques. The English Camp is still dotted with neat, white buildings, boys play football on the lush grass, and a handsome, white-haired volunteer patrols in the red-jacketed woolen uniform of the Royal Marines."

Although the Americans could be said to have won the Pig War by obtaining the San Juan Islands, any sense of victory is muted on San Juan Island, possibly because the city of Victoria, British Columbia, is clearly visible across Haro Strait.

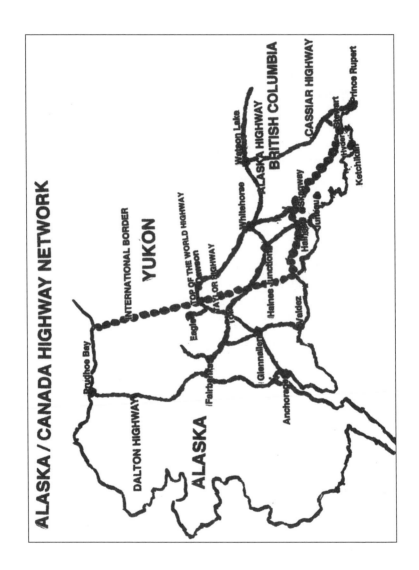

ALASKA / CANADA HIGHWAY NETWORK

# Alaska Update

Alaska has changed considerably since the Alaska-Canada Border controversy. In 1904 when the border was determined, most of the Alaska population lived in Southeastern Alaska, the old Russian American "lisiere." Gold had been discovered there in the 1880s by Joe Juneau, and the resulting town, which would soon replace the Russian-American capital of Sitka as the capital of the District of Alaska, was named for him. The only other significant Alaska population center was out on the Bering Sea at Nome, the site of the 1899 gold rush. Gold was just being discovered in the Alaska interior, leading to the settlement of Fairbanks. Copper discoveries had not yet sparked the development of the Kennecott Copper Company and the Copper River Northwestern Railroad. Alaska Railroad construction and the founding of Anchorage would not occur for over ten years. Active mining was still taking place in the Canada Klondike gold fields, Dawson was an established city and center of the Yukon territorial government.

A hundred years later, the situations are reversed. Alaska became the forty-ninth American state in 1959. The majority of Alaska's population now lives in Anchorage, Fairbanks, and the rail belt area between them. The state capital is still in Juneau although an increasing number of administrative offices have moved to Anchorage. In Canada, the Yukon is still a territory with its capital in Whitehorse. Dawson is a small town, relying primarily on summer tourism.

The area around the actual border is sparsely populated on both the American and Canada sides. People living in the border area are often dependent on each other regardless of nationality, The only area of conflict involves species that can not honor artificial borders, notably salmon. Although they may spawn in Canada's streams, they travel north to feed and mature in Alaska waters and are often caught in transit by Alaska fishermen, leading to controversy about whose fish they are.

An attempt was made in 1985 to establish levels of permissible salmon catch by Alaskan fishermen, but Canadian fishermen continued to contend that Alaskans were catching too many fish that originated in Canada, thus depleting Canada stocks. In 1995 disgruntled Canadians protested by attempting to prevent the Alaska State ferry *Taku* from docking at Prince Rupert, British Columbia.

Shortly after Alaska achieved statehood in 1959, Governor William A. Egan established a marine highway system to enable people in roadless Southeastern towns and cities to connect with a highway at Haines, Alaska on Lynn Canal and with highways in British Columbia and Washington state. Prince Rupert, British Columbia, a city with a population of about 17,000 on the trans-continental Yellowhead Highway became an important stop on the Alaska Marine Highway. In addition, tourists from both the United States and Canada discovered the Alaska ferry system as a relatively inexpensive way to visit Alaska.

The initial attack on the *Taku* lasted only several hours before allowing the egg-splattered ferry to land at Prince Rupert. Two years later, Canadian fishermen were incensed when a representative of the United States State Department admitted that 400,000 red salmon, far above the 120,000 quota, had been inadvertently caught by Alaska fishermen in nets while fishing for pink salmon. As the Alaska ferry *Malaspina* approached the dock at Prince Rupert early on the morning of Saturday, July 19, 1997, four Canadian fishing vessels attempted, unsuccessfully, to prevent it from docking. While in port for two hours, the ferry took on more passengers and vehicles. By the time the *Malaspina* was prepared to leave with 328 people and 71 vehicles on board, more fishing boats had arrived and succeeded in barricading the ferry in port. By the end of the day over 200 fishing boats had converged on Prince Rupert from ports in Canada, some as far away as Vancouver. Most of the ferry passengers were American rather than Canadian. Several left with full reimbursement, but most spent the night on board awaiting developments while local police and Canadian Mounted Police patrolled the waterfront. Four men from Olympia, Washington, on their way to a week fishing trip in Ketchikan spent the day in the *Malaspina* bar playing an appropriate game called "Screw Your Neighbor."

The following day the Alaska attorney general obtained an injunction from a court in Canada demanding that the Canadian fishermen release the *Malaspina*. By the time the ferry left Prince Rupert on Monday evening, many passengers had jumped ship with full refunds. The ferry and its remaining passengers remained in Ketchikan that night while making plans for the remainder of the trip north. The schedules of two of the three large Alaska ferries were altered and Prince Rupert was temporarily removed from their schedules. Alaska officials speculated that Hyder, Alaska, at the head of Portland Canal, might replace Prince Rupert on the Alaska Marine Highway.

The Canadian fishermen met with Canada Fishing Minister David Anderson, who arranged for bilateral meetings to re-negotiate the 1985 Salmon Treaty. Alaskan and Canadian negotiators agreed on an abundance-based management scheme by which allowable quotas could be altered during a fishing season depending on the observed return of various species of salmon. The State of Alaska sued Canada for the ferry crew's overtime pay and other expenses resulting from the blockade and received compensation consisting largely of promises to advertise Alaska tourism in Canada. Both countries were gratified that the general good relationship between Canada and Alaska precluded any violence. Prince Rupert was soon re-established as a regular port on the Alaska Marine Highway. Prospective expansion of the port at Prince Rupert will benefit trade with the Far East by cutting a day in transit for ships that usually would go to Vancouver. A recent article in the Juneau newspaper noted that enlargement of the Prince Rupert port would be a financial boon to Southeastern Alaska.

## SOUTHEASTERN ALASKA

When a Canadian anthropologist attempted to convince Dr. Judith Kleinfeld, Director of the Northern Studies Program at the University of Alaska, of the superiority of Canadian culture, she pointed to the example of the neighboring towns, Stewart, B.C. and Hyder, Alaska, at the head of Portland Canal. Dr. Kleinfeld and her husband visited these communities and registered their observations in the July 19, 2004 issue of the *Wall Street Journal*. While soliciting advance information for their 1200 mile highway trip from Fairbanks to the southernmost tip of Southeastern Alaska, the Kleinfelds discovered that Stewart was an established town with a "municipal government incorporated under the laws of the Province of British Columbia" while the American town of Hyder was not incorporated, but run by a community association of "happy people."

An initial drive through the towns after dark revealed Stewart to be a planned community with a neat grid of paved streets while Hyder, two miles away, appeared unorganized with no straight streets. On closer examination the next day, many of the quiet Victorian homes and businesses in Stewart needed paint and displayed FOR SALE signs. Hyder, on the other hand showed evidence of entrepreneurial energy with businesses including: a flourishing restaurant in a gutted school bus; the Border Bandit Discount Store, frequented by people from all over northern British Columbia and Yukon; and a glacier water bottling plant. The Canada Day celebration in Stewart on July 2 featured a rescue equipment demonstration and the Annual Community Potluck Dinner. Two days later on July 4, Hyder had an Ugly Vehicle Contest and a Wilderness Woman Contest, with contestants racing to split wood, wash clothes, shoot a bear, flip pancakes, change a baby, and put on lipstick. Several years before the Hyderites had succeeded in burning down the fire station with fireworks on the Fourth of July.

The rundown condition of buildings in Stewart is understandable considering that many date back to 1914 when the area boasted a population of 10,000. Mining ceased in 1956, with the exception of the Grand Duc Copper Mine, which operated until 1984. A local pulp mill closed when lumbering in the Tongass National Forest was restricted. The Kleinfelds noted that there was a border station and customs agents in Stewart but not in Hyder. They speculated that Stewart, needing jobs, welcomed all the customs officers and government employees it could get. They quoted Canadian sociologist Kaspar Naegele: "In Canada there seems to be greater acceptance of limitation, of hierarchical patterns. There seems to be less optimism, less faith in the future, less willingness to risk capital or reputation." (With the recent emphasis on border security, Hyder has probably now acquired more government personnel.)

In spite of the apparent difference in culture between Stewart and Hyder, they are interdependent. They share an International Chamber of Commerce website on the internet, where they boast a setting which "can only be described as amazing, combining an oceanfront location with alpine scenery, glaciers, ice fields, and spectacular waterfalls." They hope to attract tourists with fresh and saltwater fishing, boating, hiking, cross-country skiing, and snowmobiling. The spectacular scenery can be admired in the American movie *Insomnia* starring Al Pacino and Hilary Swank which was filmed in Stewart in 2004.

Stewart, with an estimated population of 700, advertises low cost available housing and land, a skilled work force, a salt water port, a large barge terminal, a paved highway, an excess of hydro power, and new sewage lagoons capable of servicing a town of 6000. Hyder, which was originally called Portland City, was named for a Canadian mining engineer. Known as the "Friendliest Ghost Town in Alaska," Hyder has grown to a population of 100 from 71 ten years ago.

Ketchikan, located on Revillagigedo Island, 90 miles north of Prince Rupert, B.C. is the southeasternmost sizable city in Alaska with a relatively stable population of about 8000. Tourism and fishing are the main industries in the area since the pulp mill shut down about twenty years ago due to restrictions on lumbering in the Tongass National Forest. The Ketchikan airport is located on nearby Gravina Island, necessitating a short ferry ride to downtown Ketchikan. Recently Ketchikan has received international notoriety as the home of the "bridge to nowhere." In 2005 the Alaska Congressional delegation succeeded in getting an earmark in the federal budget, and the Highway Bill provided $22.3 million to build a bridge from Ketchikan to Gravina Island which had very little population aside from the airport. Although this potential bridge was dear to the hearts of the people of Ketchikan, it was ridiculed by the press and some senators as an example of abuse of the earmark system of allocating federal funds. The earmark has since been altered so the bridge has not been built. A gravel road to nowhere now connects the airport to the site of a potential bridge. Ketchikan boasts ample opportunity for sport fishing and hiking, but golfers must take the ferry south to Prince Rupert or north to Wrangell where golf courses have been built on wood chips from defunct pulp mills.

The town of Wrangell, Alaska, with a population of 2,308 in the 2000 census, is located at the mouth of the Stikine River where the Hudson's Bay Company had its primary base, Fort Stikine, while renting the "lisiere" from the Russian America Company between 1840 and 1867. Wrangell is rich in history, but doesn't accommodate the large summer cruise ships that almost double the populations of Ketchikan and Juneau on the days they are in port. Wrangell is a regular stop on the Alaska Marine Highway, often in the middle of the night. The Stikine River, which used to be a regular trade route for Indians and for prospectors during the Cassiar Gold Rush, is sometimes used to transport ore from minesin Canada. Regular river boats no longer run between Wrangell and Telegraph Creek, B.C.

Canada's mines have registered interest in using Taku Inlet, near Juneau, to transport ore. A representative of Redfern Resources, the developer of the Tulsequah Chief Mine, recently gave a presentation to the Juneau Chamber of Commerce indicating that Juneau might expect an economic impact of $24 million annually when the mine begins operation in about a year. The mine is along the Tulsequah River, 13 miles upstream of the Taku River and 40 miles northeast of Juneau. Minerals from the mine would be transported down the Taku River and past Juneau to Skagway for shipment overseas. The State of Alaska, however, has some reservations about the impact of the mining on salmon in the Taku River. Alaska and Canada have different permitting procedures.

Juneau, with a 2007 estimated population of 30,000 is by far the largest city in Southeast Alaska. Mining is still active in the Juneau area with the Greens Creek Mine, owned by Hecla Mining Company, and the Kensington Gold Mine, but government is, by far, Juneau's major employer. In order to avoid a confrontation, the framers of the Alaska State Constitution purposefully avoided specifying a permanent location of the state capital in the constitution. Juneau was stated to be the capital in Article 15, Section 20, the transitional section of the constitution, so Juneau was the capital when Alaska became the 59th state in 1959. Within a year Alaskans were asked to vote on a proposal to move the capital to an area accessible by road. Juneau proponents managed to defeat that proposition and another several years later with intense lobbying efforts. However, in the early 1970s, an Alaska Airline crash at Juneau, killing more than a hundred passengers, emphasized the dangers of the approach to the Juneau airport and the possibility of having state officials killed in a plane crash. The following year, Alaskans voted to move the capital to a site on the railbelt between Anchorage and Fairbanks. Three potential sites were identified and the electorate selected a site near

Willow, Alaska. Juneau proponents, however, insisted that a bond proposition to fund the capital move be voted on. The anticipated expenditure spooked the electorate, and although Alaskans had voted to move the capital, they did not vote to pay for the move.

Juneau has continued to fight to keep the capital. Rather than raise the issue of voting to move the capital again, more government offices have relocated to Anchorage. While Sarah Palin, who lives in Wasilla, was governor, she chose to have her main office in Anchorage and keep her family in Wasilla most of the time. She went to Juneau for the legislature and ceremonial functions like the Christmas party and collected per diem while staying in her Wasilla home.

Juneau continues to lobby for a road connection to the rest of Alaska. Avalanche hazards, steep slopes, and environmental protection concerns would make construction difficult and costly. The most recent plan would still include a ferry link before reaching Skagway. Construction on the road was due to begin in 2007, but was cancelled by Sarah Palin when she became governor.

Juneau and Whitehorse, Yukon Territory, are good neighbors, although there is no transportation route between them other than the ferry from Juneau to Skagway and the Klondike Highway between Skagway and Whitehorse. They have similar populations and are both capitals of their respective state and territory. Tennis teams compete against each other, and teams from both Alaska and Canada compete in the annual relay running race between Skagway and Whitehorse. Since Juneau and Whitehorse have different weather patterns they sometimes have to share skiing opportunities. During the 2007/2008 winter when Whitehorse had very little snow, the Eaglecrest Ski Area in Juneau honored Whitehorse ski passes.

The 1904 decision that Lynn Canal and Skagway were American did little to alter the use of the port of Skagway. The narrow gauge White Pass and Yukon railway was constructed in 1898 with English money, American engineering, and Canadian contracting. The White Pass and Yukon Route became a fully integrated transportation company, operating docks, trains, stage coaches, sleighs, buses, paddlewheelers, trucks, ships, airplanes, hotels, and pipelines, providing the essential infrastructure servicing the freight and passenger needs of Yukon's population and mining industry. In their book, *The Sinking of the Princess Sophia,* Ken Coates and

Bill Morrison describe the transportation system of Interior Alaska and the Yukon in 1918: "These small communities were tied to the 'outside' by a single transportation route running from central Alaska up the Yukon River past Dawson City to Whitehorse, then to Skagway by railway. There, on the edge of the north, goods and travellers transferred to ships owned by the Canadian Pacific Railway's steamship service, or one of its competitors, for the voyage down the Inside Passage." The majority of people entering or leaving the Yukon River valley prior to the completion of the Alaska Railroad in 1923 did so by way of Dawson, Whitehorse, and Skagway. The 353 people who lost their lives in late October of 1918 when the Canadian Pacific steamship *Princess Sophia* sank after hitting Vanderbilt Reef near Juneau were not tourists, but resident families, miners, and other workers from Alaska and the Yukon going 'outside' for the winter. Many were employees of the White Pass and Yukon Route. Coates and Morrison characterize the sinking as an "international story, involving both Alaska and Yukon Territories. The ship, though Canadian, sailed from an American port and sank in American waters, many of the would-be rescuers were American; the bodies of the victims were initially taken to an American town, and then transported to burial sites across Canada and the United States."

The White Pass and Yukon railway was taken over by the United States Army and served a vital function carrying supplies for the construction of the Alcan highway during World War II. A considerable amount of repair to the railway was necessary before it could resume its peacetime functions of transporting ore and coal from Yukon mines and carrying tourists visiting Alaska and the Yukon. The White Pass management opposed the building of the Klondike Highway between Whitehorse and Skagway, and stopped running the railway when the highway was completed in 1982 and ore was no longer transported by train.

The railway was reopened in 1988 as a seasonal tourist operation. The White Pass and Yukon railway is now Alaska's most popular shore excursion, carrying over 430,000 passengers in 2005. Recently a daily record of 6,000 passengers was established. Tourists arrive at the White Pass dock on large tour ships and can immediately board trains on the dock. Tour guides herd the "ship sheep" to trains appropriate for their specific tours. Some go to the White Pass summit and immediately return to Skagway. Others connect with buses in Canada and proceed to Whitehorse and Alaska, A third group can travel by steam train to the historic gold rush camp on Lake Bennett. The WP&YR rail fleet consists of 20 diesel electric locomotives, 70 restored and replica parlor cars, and two steam locomotives. The WP&YR is featured on American Public Radio's "Great Scenic Railway Journeys" and in a nationwide one hour special entitled "Alaska's Gold Rush Train." The White Pass and Yukon Route is a wholly-owned subsidiary of Tri-White Corporation based in Toronto, Ontario, and is traded on the Toronto Stock Exchange as TWH.

In 1998 President William Jefferson Clinton of the United States and the prime minister of Canada signed declarations designating the Klondike Gold Rush International Historical Park. Park rangers from the National Park Service and Parks Canada cooperate in describing the historical significance of the area and assisting tourists hiking the Chilkoot Trail.

The population of Skagway was 862 according to the 2000 census, but it more than doubles in the summer tourist season in order to deal with more than 900,000 visitors between May and October. Some permanent residents of Skagway depend on Whitehorse for medical and dental care and use Whitehorse automotive outlets. They also frequent the Walmart and other commercial outlets in Whitehorse. Border patrol has become more of an issue with the requirement for passports when traveling through Canada. Recently ten new mobile homes have been moved to Skagway to house additional border control personnel.

Haines at the end of Chilkat inlet on the west side of Lynn Canal does not share the heavy tourist traffic during the summer, although some eco-tours come to enjoy the spectacular setting and the large eagle population. Haines' current claim to fame is a resident author. Heather Lende got her literary start writing obituaries for the local paper and subsequently has published two books containing folksy tales about her hometown where pot luck dinners are the main entertainment and high school students ride the state ferry to compete with teams in other Southeastern Alaska towns. The population of Haines varies seasonally. In her weekly column in the *Anchorage Daily News*, Lende commented: "Sidewalks are rarely passable once it snows, but there are so few of us here in the winter that it is usually safe to walk or run in the road, sometimes right down the middle."

ALONG THE 141ST PARALLEL

Marian Botsford Fraser did not attempt to walk the border between Southeastern Alaska and British Columbia undoubtedly because most of it is covered with ice and snow throughout the year. She concluded her tour of the border, however, by following the 141st parallel between Alaska and the Yukon Territory—a border never contested because it was specified in the treaty between Russia and Great Britain in 1825.

Eagle City, Alaska, nestled under Eagle Bluff on the Yukon River, was settled as a military post during the Klondike gold rush and became the center of Alaska's Third Judicial District until it was moved to Fairbanks. Miners and their families continued to use Eagle as a base and spend winters there, so Eagle, which had an estimated population of 147 in 2007, was never considered a ghost town. After 1953 when the Taylor Highway was completed connecting Eagle to the Alaska Highway, other people, some of them retired government workers, settled in Eagle, drawn by its isolation and spectacular setting. These Eagleites have taken a great interest in the historical preservation of the town and adjoining Fort Egbert, sometimes fighting the National Park Service and other times working with it to provide tours through the museums and restored buildings. New buildings in Eagle are mainly log structures that fit in with the character of the original town. Tour buses bring tourists from Fairbanks over the dusty Taylor Highway and a smattering of independent Alaska tourists endure the 100 mile drive from Tetlin junction on the Alaska Highway to attend the famous Fourth of July celebration in Eagle.

After surviving on the banks of the Yukon River for more than a century, severe ice jams on the river in the spring of 2009 almost destroyed the Eagle waterfront.

When Marian Fraser drove the Taylor Highway at the end of her trip along the border in the 1980s, she commented that the only station available on her car radio featured "a dissonant choir plaintively singing a long and tuneless song with the words, 'Jesus, Jesus', coming and going as waves of comprehensible sound in a bed of static and a chorus in the Inuit language." Anyone contemplating an automobile trip on the Taylor and Alaska highways should take a supply of audio books. The only Alaska stations transmitting in the area are religious stations in Glennallen and North Pole. Once over the border, interesting historical commentaries from a station in Whitehorse are sometimes available on the car radio.

Dawson City, the other oasis in this wilderness, can be reached by highway from Whitehorse, by river boat from Eagle, or by driving the Taylor Highway to Chicken and then the Top of the World Highway to the Yukon River, where a short ferry trip takes car and driver into Dawson. The Top of the World Highway lives up to its name, ziz-zagging from mountain top to mountain top. The narrow dirt road is not designed for camper trailers, but they regularly attempt to travel it, causing moments of concern when they meet each other traveling in opposite directions.

The slightly over a thousand residents of Dawson, like those of Eagle, have taken efforts to preserve some of the buildings from the Klondike Gold Rush and entertain tourists with nightly performances at the Palace Theatre. Marian Fraser found that "government-regulated gambling" was available at Diamond Tooth Gerties, where "toothy, full-faced young women pump and bellow their way through songs like 'Frankie and Johnnie'." Dawson and the surrounding area draw about 60,000 tourists a year, mostly by tour bus, far fewer than pass through Skagway and Whitehorse. A residual amount of mining is the other economic activity in the area.

A world-famous activity, linking Whitehorse and Dawson in the Yukon with Eagle and Fairbanks in Alaska, is the Yukon Quest, a thousand mile international sled dog race, held each February since 1984. The race runs from Whitehorse to Fairbanks in odd-numbered years, and from Fairbanks to Whitehorse in even-numbered years. A single musher and a team of 12 to 14 sled dogs race for 10 to 14 days, following the historic Klondike Gold Rush and river mail delivery routes. The mushers, who must pack up to 250 pounds of equipment and provisions for themselves and the dogs, are permitted to drop dogs at checkpoints, but are not allowed to replace the sled or accept help until they reach the halfway point at Dawson City. The race route runs on frozen rivers, across open water and bad ice and over four mountain ranges, reaching an elevation of 3,800 feet. Temperatures during the race can drop to as low as -40 to -60 F with winds that reach up to 100 miles per hour. Winners are usually from Alaska or the Yukon. This race is not as well known as the Iditarod Race, which is run in early March along the historic Iditarod Trail from Anchorage, Alaska to Nome, Alaska. In 2007 and 2008, Lance

Mackey, an Alaskan musher from Fairbanks won both the Yukon Quest and the Iditarod in the same year.

Highways cross the border in only two places, on the Top of the World Highway and near Beaver Creek on the Alaska Highway. Once in Canada there are two routes to the rest of the United States, the Alaska Highway to Dawson Creek, British Columbia, and the Cassiar Highway, which follows the border more closely, ending near Prince Rupert, British Columbia, with a side road to Stewart, British Columbia, and Hyder, Alaska. Travelers heading to the west coast states usually take the Cassiar Highway.

Marian Botsford Fraser commented on the cultural difference between Americans and Canadians along this remote, sparsely-populated northern boundary from her Canadian point of view. "For Canadians, the Yukon is part of our collective self-image as Northerners; there is a simple logic in our fantasies, extending from the 49th parallel in the south right through to the Arctic. It is similar to the nineteenth-century American dream of Manifest Destiny, except that it does not for the most part express itself in settlement, or even in exploration. It derives from our first exposure as schoolchildren to big red maps of the Dominion of Canada, which indelibly printed in our minds a sense of nationhood extending unimpeded to the North Pole. There are no barriers between the rest of Canada and our northern territories. In contrast, Alaskans have a sharp sense of themselves as being apart from the rest of their country, which they call the Lower Forty-Eight. There are regular calls for independence, a loathing for the federal bureaucracy and a beleaguered sense of being a misunderstood, different society (not so much a society as a far-flung penal colony of irascible individuals). Alaska is an island for intolerant Americans, especially in those communities remote from urban centres or close to the Canada border."

Fraser's generalization is unjustly critical of Alaskans, but she does have a point. Not being contiguous with the "south 48," those of us who are long-time Alaskans and can remember the fight for statehood fifty years ago do have a more solid connection with our state than most other Americans have with their respective states. We sing the Alaska Flag Song more frequently and with as much reverence as the Star Spangled Banner and we hang the Alaska flag along with an American flag on patriotic days. However, calls for independence are scarcely heard since we became the 49th state. Fraser was probably influenced during her travel through this sparsely-populated region by meeting people with the "end of the road syndrome," which has motivated anti-social people to get as far away from organized society as possible. She cites John McPhee's book *Coming Into the Country* in which he describes the dissatisfaction that residents of Eagle, Alaska and environs felt with federal land withdrawals, occasioned by the Alaska National Interest Lands Act (ANILCA) which established the Yukon Charley National Preserve in the 1980s. Fraser sums it up, "44 million acres were given the natives in the Alaska Native Claims Settlement, and 80 million acres were designated for federal wildlife and recreational reserves. The Alaskan homesteader, with only 250 million acres left in which to roam, felt trapped."

# Future

The United States has fared well in past border negotiations with Great Britain and Canada, particularly when considering that territory close to the border would have been comparatively more valuable to Canada where most of the population lives within 200 miles of the border with the United States. There still are border controversies today that need resolution. On both coasts relatively minor controversies are related to fishing rights.

On the east coast, the Machias Seal Island, a 20-acre island at the mouth of the Bay of Fundy between Maine and New Brunswick, lies in a gray zone in which both the United States and Canada are permitted to fish. Conflict between lobstermen results from differences in regulations between the two countries. For example, as noted in the October 13, 2007 issue of *The Economist*, the United States prohibits taking large lobsters that have reproductive value, but allows more traps than Canada in the crowded area. The island is uninhabited except for one or two Canadian lighthouse keepers, who maintain the lighthouse placed on the island in 1832. The island is a nesting ground for Atlantic puffins and both countries run bird watching tours to the island, which the government in Canada has proclaimed to be a bird sanctuary. On the west coast at Dixon Entrance between British Columbia and Alaska, the A-B line, established in the 1904 boundary settlement agreement, touches the Alaska islands in two places. Alaska has protested that it was not allotted territorial waters and fishing rights in these locations.

A more serious border controversy is in the Beaufort Sea. The 1825 treaty between Russia and Great Britain established the 141st parallel as the boundary only as far as the Arctic coast. Canada and the United States disagree on where the border should be in the Beaufort Sea, Canada advocating a straight extension of the 141st parallel while the

United States would bend the border to the east. With the potential of oil and gas discovery in the offshore land and ocean bottom, establishment of the boundaries could become an important international imperative. Recently Russia has proclaimed ownership of the North Pole. Denmark and Norway also have claims on offshore arctic lands.

With yearly decrease in arctic ice, it is possible that a northwest passage for shipping will soon be open at least in the summer. Since the islands surrounding a potential northwest passage are Canada's, Canada believes it should own the route, while the United States advocates international ownership. Security and control of a potential northwest sea route is a future consideration.

In future negotiations with Canada, the United States should give recognition to the differences in American and Canadian culture. Americans, particularly those not living close to the northern border, have little understanding of Canada's history and do not realize that the border has a special significance to Canadians. Until the increase in border security after September 11, 2001, Americans didn't really consider Canada to be a foreign country and gave little thought to crossing the border. For Canadians, on the other hand, as pointed out by Marian Fraser, the border is a "holding line, a sea wall, sandbags resisting America. The waters slapping against the sandbags are not threatening, but when we contemplate the potential force of the body behind them, in full flood, we take silent comfort in the sandbags."

Now the United States is putting up more sandbags of its own, with the result that lines are long at border crossings. Canada, in particular, is concerned about restriction of trade. Both countries are developing mechanisms by which people who need to cross the border frequently can avoid unnecessary delay. However, Janet Napolitano, the United States Homeland Security secretary, makes no apologies for the tightened security measures, including using unmanned Predator aircraft to patrol the border with Canada. At a recent conference on the northern border at the Brookings Institution, Secretary Napolitano, who previously was governor of Arizona, stated, "One of the things that I think we need to be sensitive to is the very real feeling among southern border states, and in Mexico, that if things are being done on the Mexican border, they should also be done on the Canada border." However, problems like illegal immigration on the Mexican border are not problems on the northern border that require strict measures like fencing. Although security measures are being enhanced, Canada hopes to have problems of delay at the border resolved when Vancouver, British Columbia hosts the winter Olympic Games in 2010. It is ironical that, in Europe, nations with differing ethnic backgrounds are removing barriers, while, in North America, nations with the same ethnic origin are creating them.

Most Americans still do not think of Canadians as foreigners—they are our cousins, often literally as well as figuratively, our alter egos and our conscience. Canadian historian Pierre Berton, who grew up in Dawson City and studied the comparison of American mining camps ruled by miners' meeting with Canadian camps under surveillance by the Royal Canadian Mounted Police, summed up the cultural difference during a meeting of the International Symposium on Mining in Fairbanks, Alaska in September 1997. "I know Americans sometimes irritate Canadians by saying, 'Oh, you're just like we are.' Well, we aren't you know, and we know it. We speak the same language, we wear the same clothes and watch a lot of the same movies. But there is an enormous difference between us. This all came out along the trails to the gold camps. I already became aware of the difference when I did my research on the Klondike Gold Rush. First, of course, in Canada, we did not separate formally from Europe. We are one of the few countries that didn't have a revolution. So the history may be a bit less interesting, but there are fewer graves along the way. Historically, the United States, you can easily see this when you study the Klondike, is a revolutionary nation, a nation of individuals, and of revolutionary individuals. Canada is a nation created by the British Colonial System. It's a part of us, just as the Revolution and the Civil War are part of you. So the Canadian quite often puts order before freedom, while the American tends to put freedom before order. Of course order, in its most extreme, can lead to repression, and that has happened. But freedom can also lead to license and that also has happened. … It is the U.S. style, I think, to elect just about everybody including judges and lawmen. Canadians appoint people from the top down to the grass roots. Americans elect people from the bottom up, from the grass roots."

# Bibliographical Notes

## TREATY OF PARIS

No special sources were used for the factual material about the American Revolution and the Treaty of Paris. American children are exposed in childhood to books about children living in the American colonies during the American Revolution in the American Girl and the Dear America series, but rarely to books that describe the life of Loyalist children. When I learned that there was a Dear Canada Scholastic Series, I decided to read some of the books. *With Nothing But Our Courage, The Loyalist Diary of Mary MacDonald* by Karleen Bradford tells a moving story about a Loyalist family resettling in Upper Canada from upstate New York. I recommend this book to give middle school children and even adults some appreciation of the other side of the American Revolution.

## WAR OF 1812 and TREATY OF GHENT

Several excellent sources were used to gain an understanding of the importance of the War of 1812 for both Canada and the United States. My initial interest in Canada's history resulted from reading Pierre Berton's two-volume history of the War of 1812, *The Invasion of Canada, 1812-1813* and *Flames Across the Border 1813-1814*. These books give a story of the war that differs from the presentation I received in American history classes. If these books are difficult to find in the United States, they are readily available, new or used, on Amazon. To balance the Canadian interpretation, I read two recent American books, *1812, The War That Forged a Nation* by Walter R. Borneman, Harper Perennial, 2004, and *Union 1812* by A.J. Langguth, Simon and Schuster, 2006. The Langguth book consists mainly of biographical sketches of some American participants in the war—Isaac Brock is the only British general included. The Borneman book, on the other hand, gives an excellent chronological account of the war that, though not as detailed as the Berton books, tells essentially the same story, but with more emphasis on the importance to the United States of the Battle of New Orleans, which actually took place after the signing of the Treaty of Ghent. *The Naval War of 1812* by Theodore Roosevelt gives excellent detailed accounts of the naval battles in which the American navy excelled. This book, initially published by Putnam, New York, in 1882, was republished in 1999 by De Capo Press. The Dear Canada Series book *Whispers of War, The War of 1812 Diary of Susan Merritt*, is based on the life of a girl living on the Niagara front.

## FORTY-NINTH PARALLEL and OREGON TREATY

My Canada source for these chapters is *Caesars in the Wilderness,* the second volume of Peter C. Newman's three volume history of the Hudson's Bay Company, Penquin Books, Canada. Prior to reading the Newman books, I was unaware of the part that the Hudson's Bay Company played in the history of the American as well as the Canadian west. My American source is *For Honor or Destiny, The Anglo-American Crisis over the Oregon Territory* by Donald A. Rakestraw, American University Studies, Peter Lang, New York, 1995, which deals with the political maneuvering involved in the eventual compromise and the historical background of the claims that the United States and Great Britain had to the Oregon territory.

## AROOSTOCK WAR and WEBSTER-ASHBURTON TREATY

I was fortunate to have contact with John Bransom, an Alaska historian who is a descendant of John Baker, one of the original American settlers in the upper St. Johns River valley of Maine. He lent me his copy of *Ties of Common Blood, A History of Maine's Boundary Dispute with Great Britain, 1783-1842* by Geraldine Tidd Scott, Heritage Books, Bowie, Md. 1992. Bransom also put me in contact with a cousin currently living in the area. *Ties of Common Blood* is a detailed account of the period with excerpts from primary sources. Because of his participation in resolving this conflict as well as participating in the War of 1812 and later mediating the Pig War, I consulted *Agent of Destiny, The Life and Times of General Winfield Scott* by John S.D. Eisenhower. Another source that provides accounts of related eastern border conflicts such as the *Caroline* affair on the Niagara peninsula in addition to the Aroostock War is *The Crisis of 1830-1842 in Canadian-American Relations,* by Albert B. Corey, Russell and Russell, New York, 1970.

## PIG WAR
*The Pig War, Standoff at Griffin Bay* by Michael Vouri, Griffin Bay Bookstore, Friday Harbor, WA.,2006, is a detailed history of this conflict written by a ranger at the local National Park. Michael Vouri has also written *Outpost of Empire, The Royal Marines and the Joint Occupation of San Juan Island,* Northwest Interpretive Association, Seattle, 2004, which provides information on the reconstruction of English Camp.

## ALASKA BORDER CONFLICT
The most comprehensive and readable book on the Alaska border controversy is *Boundary Hunters* by Lewis Green, UBC Press, Vancouver, 1982, which covers both the 1904 Tribunal, which resolved the boundary dispute, and the history leading up to the conflicting claims. In addition, this book tells the story of the difficult job actually marking the border. *The Alaska Boundary Dispute* edited by John A. Munro, Issues in Canadian History, Toronto, 1970, contains excerpts on the subject from varies magazines and books, including: *The Alaska Boundary* by Hon. John W. Foster from *The National Geographic Magazine* Vol.X, November 1899, No.11, pp.452-456 and quotations from the Canadian press following the boundary award. *The Alaska Border Dispute, A Critical Reappraisal* by Norman Penlington , McGraw Hill Ryerson Ltd., Toronto, 1972, is another analysis of the subject. *The Alaskan Boundary Tribunal* by Hon. John W. Foster, LLD, *The National Geographic Magazine* Vol.XV, No. 1, January, 1904, was written while the Tribunal was in session. *When Russia Was in America* by Mykhaylo Huculak, Mitchell Press Limited, Vancouver, gives an analysis of factors surrounding the 1825 treaty between Russia and Great Britain upon which the border controversy was based.

## THE BORDER TODAY and ALASKA UPDATE
If I had been able to actually visit many of the places along the border, I would have done so. I was fortunate to find *Walking the Line, Travels Along the Canadian/American Border* by Marian Botsford Fraser, Sierra Club Books, San Francisco, 1989. Fraser actually visited many places along the border. On places I could not visit, I utilized some of her observations, which were valuable because they reflected a Canadian point of view. *Beauty Tips From Moose Jaw, Travels in Search of Canada,* by Will Ferguson, Albert A. Knopf. Canada, 2004, also has some interesting descriptions of border localities, particularly along the Maine/New Brunswick border. Ferguson, a Canadian humorist, is not above poking fun at both Canadians and Americans.

# Index

125